T0164213

Shivitti: the eighth verse from the sixteenth Psalm,
"I have set the Lord always before me."

SHIVITTI: A Vision

BY THE SAME AUTHOR

Atrocity

House of Dolls

Kaddish

Phoenix Over the Galilee

Piepel

Salamandra

Star Eternal

Sunrise Over Hell

K.Z. (German pronunciation ka-tzet) are the initials of *Konzentration Zenter* (Concentration Camp). Every K.Z. inmate was known as "KaTzetnik Number ...," the number itself branded into the flesh of the left arm. The author of *Shivitti* was KaTzetnik 135633.

[E.D'M.A.]

SHIVITTI
A Vision

KA-TZETNIK 135633

TRANSLATED FROM THE HEBREW
BY ELIYAH NIKE DE-NUR AND
LISA HERMAN

Gateways Consciousness Classics

Gateways / IDHHB Publishers
Nevada City, California

Originally published in Hebrew by Hakibbutz Hameuchad Publishing House Ltd., 1987. All translations from the Hebrew Bible are by the author.

First U.S. edition published as *SHIVITTI: A Vision* by Harper & Row, Publishers, Inc., 1989.

SHIVITTI: A Vision. English translation copyright © 1998 by Yehiel De-Nur. First Gateways edition published September, 1998.
ISBN: 978-0-89556-113-8

Gateways edition typeset by Lily Nova.
Cover design by Nancy Christie & Marvette Kort.

This publishing project manifested due to the inspiration, dedication, and hard work of Reza Leah Landman, with help and support from Cynthia Merchant. Gateways would also like to thank the following contributors: Cathy and Rob Calef of Open Secret Bookstore, San Rafael, California, for their special fund-raising efforts; the Multidisciplinary Association for Psychedelic Studies (MAPS) for project support and publicity; and all the other individuals who with goodwill and an open heart donated towards the publication of this edition.

Library of congress cataloging-in-publication data
Ka-tzetnik 135633, 1917-
[Tsofen. English]
Shivitti : a vision / Ka-tzetnik 135633 ; translated from the Hebrew by Eliyah Nike De-Nur and Lisa Herman.
   p.   cm.
Previously published : 1ˢᵗ U.S. ed. San Francisco : Harper & Row, c1989
   ISBN 0-89556-113-1 (pbk.)
   1.   Ka-tzetnik, 135633, 1917- --Imprisonment. 2. Holocaust, Jewish (1939-1945) -- Personal narratives. 3. Auschwitz (Concentration camp) 4. Authors, Israeli --Biography.   I. Title.
   PJ5054.K343Z47713   1998
   892.4'36 --dc21   98-42908
                                  CIP

TABLE OF CONTENTS

Claudio Naranjo (left) with the author, reading the manuscript of Shivitti
Berkeley, CA — 1986

PREFACE

We have here a little book of immense bearing, which might well be announced in terms similar to those chosen by a reviewer of the recent movie on the sinking of the Titanic. Just as in his review he observed that the moviegoer should not come to admire such things as camera work or even plot, but to grasp the enormity of the event that was reflected by the movie—here the reader should not look so much for literature, psychotherapy, or history as for the extremity of the experience of the holocaust.

Before all else we should be aware of the rarity of this document. Not only was it exceptional enough for the author to survive Auschwitz, but it is a rare thing for someone who has undergone such a descent into hell to be able to tell the story. Furthermore, I am sure that most human beings don't even succeed in being truly present to themselves before such horror, while here we have still another striking exception: De-Nur is able to be a witness in retrospect because he was an exceptional witness of life at its worst, *while it was happening*. It is precisely to this that we may attribute his very survival—or more exactly, to the fact that he was able to keep the *Shivitti* (i.e. the reminder of the presence of God) always before him throughout his years of imprisonment.

Beyond all that, this is a more exceptional book than a simple memoir would have been. That had been accomplished already by De-Nur under his pseudonym (Ka-tzetnik 135633) in his earlier book *Salamandra*, driven by a sense of mission in reporting what he had lived. The present volume is, rather, a report on hell revisited, i.e. one on the experience of dealing *again* with his scarcely bearable memories in order to heal from them and so to regain a peace of mind after thirty years of sleeplessness and nightmares.

As I write this I am reminded of what I once heard a South American shaman say concerning courage. "There is the courage of ordinary warriors," he said, "who risk their lives in battle, and there is the greater courage required for the inner adventure of ingesting 'teaching plants' that are part of a healer's training." If it was already a heroic feat for De-Nur to have been able to survive physically through an exceptional spiritual aliveness, an additional heroism was involved in his willingness to return to Auschwitz decades later under the effect of LSD.

I consider it a great privilege that Mr. De-Nur has asked me to write this preface to his very remarkable book, and take pleasure in feeling that I am the right person for it. I not only know but feel great regard for the three persons involved in his narrative: De-Nur himself, his wife Eliyah (here Nike), and my colleague Dr. Bastiaans. Rather than commenting any further on a book that speaks for itself, I want to end this preface with some reflection on the deliberately ignored usefulness of LSD and other psychedelics in psychotherapy.

Having been one of the very few (along with Dr. Bastiaans and Dr. Grof) privileged to receive institutional support for clinical research in this field, I had occasion to draw the world's attention in the sixties to the extraordinary potential of substances that I then proposed to call *feeling enhancers* (now re-baptized *empathogens*) and *fantasy enhancers* (or oneirophrenics). Having had the opportunity to ascertain that these constituted something akin to psychological lubricants that make it possible to offer therapeutic help to some beyond the possibility of being reached effectively, I have naturally been sorry for the unfortunate way in which politics has interfered with the precious healing potential of psychedelics in psychotherapy. With the enlightened exception of the Netherlands and Switzerland, psychedelics are regarded today as dangerous drugs without any usefulness, and thus rendered useless through prohibition. I cannot help but feel that in times of global crisis when it becomes clear that our very survival is endangered by our obsolete patterns of relationship to self and others, and when our highest hope lies in the *human factor*, we allow ourselves to scorn such a powerful and timely therapeutic resource! It is true that some individuals are addiction prone and that addiction is a sizable social problem in our midst; yet it is no less true that addiction arises from improper drug use, and improper drug use is fostered by a social situation in which the constructive potential of drugs is thwarted.

I hope that the time comes when LSD and other therapeutically useful substances can be controlled (like morphine and the amphetamines) and yet put to good use by experts, and when schools arise for the transmission of expertise from the living few to a new generation of practitioners.

Because of this I hope that this book not only conveys De-Nur's spiritual accomplishment and human understanding, but also speeds up the recognition of a form of psychotherapy that could be helping many if it were not for a questionable prohibitionism that is part of an excessively tough minded and puritanical Establishment. I consider this prohibitionism part of a truly evil aspect of our society, and I do not see great difference between the mind-set of those who persecuted Jews at the time of World War II and that of those who invoke morality to wage today's "war on drugs." Today, as ever, the foremost characteristic of the Adversary is that of pointing away from himself to say *"There* is the Devil!"

Claudio Naranjo, M.D.
Brasilia, May 22, 1998

FOREWORD

(Prof. Bastiaans recording:)
*LSD treatment of Mr. De-Nur,
at my clinic,
Psychiatric Department,
State University of Leiden,*

July 8, 1976.

I lay naked in bed. I could still see Prof. Bastiaans's broad back as he set up the recorder near the window. I could still hear the words that prefaced each of our LSD sessions.

The room where I lay was quite spacious. By the window opposite me twilight lingered, while the room was already steeped in darkness.

There was a small table and a chair by my bed. The nurse had left a bottle and glass for the professor and then, with hushed steps, vanished from the room. I was alone in the dimness, alone with Prof. Bastiaans.

I didn't know why my knees were trembling. It was as if a long-sealed passageway, deep within me, had burst open and a tidal wave of horror was breaking over me, the way it had that other time. Perhaps it was a succession of events that unleashed this wave: being called by my own name, waiting naked to see eyeball to eyeball the most horrifying of all my fears—the secret revealed; the secret of the nightmares that had visited me night after night these last thirty years.

When Nike, my lifemate, heard that a psychiatrist in Holland, Professor Bastiaans-discoverer of the Concentration Camp Syndrome[1]—had been healing camp survivors with a new method of treatment incorporating LSD, she came rushing to me with this piece of good news.

I will never forget the way she suffered silently through my nightmares, concealing her own feelings. My own strangled cries would awaken me, feverish and dripping, with Nike by my side, toweling away the fearsome seepage of sweat, her eyes brimming with unspoken fear and compassion.

To this day there's this one thing I can't understand: why the nightmare never took over when I slept during the day. That is why I practically turned day into night, and night into day.

"Your suffering is over, my love!"

How completely I understood her enthusiasm. All the pain of her empathy, the suppressed agony which she had kept choked inside her for so many years now turned into gushing joy at the prospect of my salvation. I held her in my arms, not knowing how to explain to her that Prof. Bastiaans couldn't possibly help me. Prof. Bastiaans was never in Auschwitz. And even those who were there don't know Auschwitz. Not even someone who was there two long years, as I was. Auschwitz is another planet, while we humankind, occupants of planet Earth, have no key to decipher the code name Auschwitz. How dare I commit sacrilege by trifling with those eyes on their way to the crematorium? They knew where they were going. I knew where they were going. The eyes of the one crossing over boring into the eyes of the one remaining behind. The sky silent overhead, the earth silent underfoot. Only a meeting of eyes and a last silence, the inaudible tread of their feet. For naked and barefoot they went to the crematorium.

---

[1] called the K.Z. Syndrome.

For two long years they trod through me, their eyes penetrating mine. And time there, on planet Auschwitz, was not like time here. Each moment there revolved around the cogwheels of a different time-sphere.

Hell-years last longer than light-years.

They left me behind with their gaze sunk in mine. Wouldn't it be a desecration of that silent gaze if I delivered it up to Prof. Bastiaans at the Psychiatric Department in Leiden?

The next two years Nike struggled tirelessly to persuade me. Though she was at Esalen, in California, pursuing her studies in theology, she never stopped her long-distance phone pleas to me in Israel to go to Prof. Bastiaans in Holland. She plied me with books, all on one sole topic: LSD! I'd sit staring at the piles of books, whose one message to me was her pain. The pain of a loved one, at times tougher to bear than one's own.

The photograph that I had clipped out of a magazine years ago and hung in a frame over my desk–now suddenly I couldn't tear my eyes away from it, away from the face of the Jew in his tallith[2] and tefillin[3] who had been posed against a background of guffawing German soldiers as a

---

[2] *tallith:* prayer shawl.
[3] *tefillin* phylacteries: two small, square leather boxes containing parchment inscribed with scriptural passages, fastened by leather straps to the head and left arm.

souvenir of the event. For the first time I took note that the normally square case of the head tefillin was spread into three peaks, like the three strokes in the Hebrew letter *sheen* (**שׁ**), and was perched like a crown on the head of the Jew. He was about my age. Any moment now a bullet would dispatch him to join the row of corpses lined at the feet of the rollicking German fraternity of warriors. But it was not the moment of shooting that was of significance here. Anyone could see this, once in touch with the hidden light radiating from the face of the Jew. Only in Auschwitz was I permitted to see this hidden light face-to-face—in the sealed isolation barracks, stuffed with human skeletons waiting for the crematorium to be cleared to receive us. And I stood, then, shoved against the Rabbi of Shilev. In the ghetto, the rabbi opposed—in the name of the Torah— armed rebellion against the Germans, arguing that such rebellion would entail certain death: suicide, which, the Rabbi said, the Torah prohibits.

It was in the eyes of the Rabbi of Shilev, as we awaited our turn for the crematorium, that I saw this same hidden light.

I couldn't tear my eyes away from the Jew on the wall. So many times had I been in his situation, but never had I attained such a state of transcendence. For in moments like this I panicked; and moments of panic are not subject to emanations of such godly light. Just look at the serenity on his face! And at those eyes, the way he looks down at the spot where he will fall in another moment! His hands are folded, defying description, as does the light beaming from his bare feet.

I stared at the piles of books that Nike had sent me from California. I had read every single one of them, but nothing hit the mark except for the one thought running through them all and now finally permeating my mind: this window I was standing by and the wall framing it—the two formed a physical barrier. Nevertheless, I could actually look through the window and observe what was happening on the other side, despite the physical barrier that it imposed.

LSD might be just that window that opens our range of vision beyond the limit that our state of consciousness has set, providing one treats the drug with the same reverence that the high priests in the temples of antiquity had for the *urim ve-tumim*[4]. For its abuse will incur the wrath of the gods.

And so, standing by the window, I landed at the threshold of resolution: perhaps it would be possible to use the LSD window to see that which was beyond the curtain dropped over my mind's eye. In other words, was the key to my nightmares to be found in the LSD code, namely in the hands of Prof. Bastiaans?

Prof. Bastiaans was tall and broad-boned with a round head fringed with burnished hair, his office as solid and inviting as his person. The walls all around were laden with books and among the volumes in Dutch translation, my own books stared out at me.

We sat, Nike and I, at a round table in the middle of the room. "Prof. Bastiaans," I made the opening move, "before we go any further I'd appreciate your understanding that I have not come here as a patient, but because I've heard that you hold a key to a gate that I've been trying to get through. So please open that gate for me, but once I'm in, kindly leave me there on my own, to myself."

I said no more. I looked into Prof. Bastiaans's experienced eyes and knew he understood.

---

[4] *urim ve-tumim:* Oracular gems set in the breastplate of the High Priest.

SHIVITTI

GATE ONE

מָה אַתָּה רֹאֶה? וָאֹמַר אֲנִי רֹאֶה מְגִלָּה עָפָה
זכריה, ה,ב

What seest thou?
And I answered: I see
a flying scroll.

ZECHARIAH 5:2

GATE ONE

(Prof. Bastiaans recording:)
LSD treatment of Mr. De-Nur,
Session One,
at my clinic,
Psychiatric Department,
State University, Leiden,

July 8, 1976.

Prof. Bastiaans switched on the recorder as he ran through his routine preamble. Falling daylight had made room for shadows. I lay naked in bed and my legs trembled. I knew what had brought me to Leiden; I knew what I must confront once and for all. But there, on the threshold of that confrontation, the horror that seized me was far worse than what I had experienced back then, there where the nightmare was reality. Suddenly I wanted to shout: "Not yet, Prof. Bastiaans, not yet!" That's how afraid I was of what was about to be revealed to me.

But rather than the shout, "Not yet!" the four Hebrew letters E.D'M.A. came crying inaudibly. That unvoiced combination was again trying to break loose, as it had every time death confronted me in Auschwitz; that mute shout again got no further than my clenched teeth. Indeed, that was the secret of its power: its potency was never dissipated, it was never exposed to the air. It was an undying flame locked within me. Dr. Mengele saw it in my eyes. It stopped him from lifting

3

his index finger to signal his subordinates to slot me with the others. "Crematorium!" He appeared stunned that the bony eye-sockets of a mussulman[1] could burn with a look like that. Naked skeletons by the hundreds were stood in line behind me, and by the time Dr. Mengele regained his composure, I had been shoved aside by his subordinates. Tick-tock, tick-tock, time is short. Hundreds more in line, waiting.

Two long years in a fiery planet called Auschwitz. Countless *Selektions.* Countless deaths. And I survived them all by finding refuge in the hush of those four Hebrew letters. I still believe it was their unvoiced power that saw me through Auschwitz. In 1945, still wrapped in the striped shrouds of an Auschwitz inmate, I first committed a description of Auschwitz to paper in *Salamandra.* It was then that my hand wrote E.D'M.A. of its own accord next to the book's title. Since then, these four Hebrew letters have headed every one of my books, in every translation, next to the title on the first page. Invariably, I am asked for the meaning of these four Hebrew letters. And I have no answer; would anyone believe me if I said these four letters kept me alive for two years on Auschwitz, planet of death?

I watched Professor Bastiaans approach me, syringe in hand. The impending sense of danger returned. Did I have the strength to face the nightmare again?

Suddenly_____
all the lights go on. Lights unlike any I've ever seen. Lights within me, behind my eyeballs, blinding me from within, as if catapulting echoes of a voice from on high:

---

[1] *musselman:* concentration camp inmate whose skin was all that held his bones together.

"Mr. De-Nur, no need for you to shake so. Please turn toward the wall, Mr. De-Nur."

The words reach my ears as if from a previous life.

And I am four years old, sitting with the other kids in heder[2], my eyes on the rabbi at the head of the table. He glows as he bends over the Torah open in front of him, teaching us about the light of the seven days of creation. His face keeps changing: one moment it looks the way it is stored in my memory, the next like the prayer-shawled Jew in the magazine clipping over my desk. They'll shoot him in the back of the head once they've shot his picture. But before he falls among the dead lined up on the ground, the horizons suddenly flare blue into other-worldly incandescences such as I've never seen.

Our rabbi's sidecurls are a bouncing phosphorescence, while we little ones are translucent, ethereal, floating. If I choose, I could now fly away on those lights and spin off to the horizon. But I like it where I am, across from the rabbi. Amazing joy fills me, and I no longer need to fly to the lights on the horizon: they're right here with me, I'm in them. The lights as well as the horizon hover about us while our rabbi keeps chanting verses from Genesis:

"And the heaven and the earth were finished, and all the host of them..."

And I, overwhelmed, see the words emerging from the rabbi's mouth. I never knew it was possible to see words made of

---

[2] *heder:* Orthodox day-school

sound. The letters are coal-black against white fire.

A magician is here to perform in my hometown's Kosciuszko Square. My nursemaid Marisha holds me up so that I can get a better view. A large crowd watches the magician begin his act by pouring huge amounts of water down his throat. He then swallows a slew of frogs and, pulling one frog after another out of his mouth, makes his grand finale. The rabbi's words, however, flow from his mouth unmanipulated, without his calling our attention to them. And the words smolder, coal-black against white fire.

"...and on the seventh day God finished..."

Suddenly the lights go out, and I am more frightened than the other kids because I can touch the darkness. Darkness is in my mouth. I can taste it. I sense darkness on my palate as if it were a thing I put in my mouth. I can't see the rabbi, but I know that he's there in his place and that he is within me. And I cry out: "Rabbi! Rabbi! Why? Why the dark?"

"Hush, hush," the rabbi's voice rebounds from the darkness within me, "There is a blackout!"

"Why is there a blackout, Rabbi?"

"Because there is a war between Man and the Serpent."

"Why is there a war, Rabbi?"

"Because it was so decreed."

"Why was it so decreed? Who decreed, Rabbi? Who decreed?"

"Ask God."

"God! God! God!"

"Who do you see, Mr. De-Nur? What do you see? Speak, tell me—"

The voice is carried from far away and comes to me. It is not dark outside at Auschwitz; there's a thick green light. The gates of the barracks are opened and we stumble out– just as we did when the doors of the cattle cars slid open onto the Auschwitz train platform. The barracks is packed with human skeletons, far beyond its capacity.

I look up into the Auschwitz skies and see the Auschwitz night receding, leaving the colors of Auschwitz in its wake for the Auschwitz day to replace it. I see the steps of the approaching day and its face, and I see the receding steps of night and its back. And within this not-day not-night, the trucks wait. The trucks are waiting for us in front of the barracks on either side of the gates that are flung open for us.

"Raus! Rraus!! Out!!"

The shouts of the kapos, barrack chiefs and barrack orderlies—"Schneller! Schneller! Hurry up! Hurry up!"—no longer faze us. We drag ourselves along. I see a river of skeletons. One naked noiseless body of skeletons, flawlessly acquiescent, flowing into the maw of the truck myself among them. If only I could lift my head a bit. Air!...A gulp of air! I'm choking, I'm drowning. Air! Air! Air!

"What are you feeling, Mr. De-Nur? Let me in, Mr. De-Nur, Tell—"

The tailgate hangs open. We hoist ourselves up onto the truck, which is here to deliver us to the crematorium. We know, of course we know. These trucks. We had seen them and known where they were going— their ceaseless back-and-forth—long before we were reduced to creatures whose will has been completely drained from their veins: mussulmen. Only this time it's our turn. It is the order of things on this planet. The back of night, the face of day. And, the trucks. And we. And Auschwitz. And within us, the crematorium. Till your turn comes. It's nature's way here.

The truck's tailgate hangs down, and we do our utmost to hoist ourselves up into it. It isn't easy for us, but we try. Anyone can see how hard we're trying. Why are the kapos and barrack chiefs screaming and swinging clubs? I don't know if the others understand, but this time I do. The screams and the clubs are not meant to prod us; no longer does the threat of clubs speed us up. Their screams are for the benefit of the S.S. officer who, by this planet's law and perfect order, must stand where he is to oversee the departure of both truck and load.

Why all the shouting and swinging of clubs over our heads? Wouldn't it make more sense for them to lend a hand to a skeleton struggling so hard to fight his way up onto the truck?

This time I can already see what's in store for me, what's about to happen inside this truck. I already see myself curling up inside the coalbin deep inside this giant truck and hiding there. This time I know it all; I just don't know why. "Rabbi, why?" I clutch at the Rabbi of Shileve with both hands. "At last you must admit, Rabbi, that God of the Diaspora himself is climbing into this truck–a mussulman."

I see the face of God hiding in a cloud. And God's face, like the Rabbi of Shilev's, is scrofulously mottled with an odd rash. His skin flakes away, like the dry, scaly bark of a withering tree. Now I clearly see the colors of the flakes: bright green, pink, and yellow. "What did you say, my son?" The Rabbi of Shilev looks up. "I said that no one will ever breathe life into these bones again. We've sinned, Rabbi. In the ghetto you opposed our uprising. Confess now: we've sinned!"

"Can't you see, my son, how even now Jacob is wrestling with the angel for our redemption? Why, we are the sinew of his thigh-bone in this struggle! Be strong, my son, this is the moment you must be strong!"

"For whom, Rabbi, does Jacob struggle with the angel, if his children are being carted off to the crematorium by the truckload? For whom, Rabbi, for whom?"

"Rrrraus! Rrrraus!!!"

Outside of the block Auschwitz is altogether different from the one I have known so well–as intimately as my own skeleton. The electrified barbed wire is magnified as under the eye of a microscope, ten thousand times its normal size. The light of this Auschwitz dawn has substance to it, and I can reach out and touch it with my hand. Metallic cobalt-blue light. The same truck I had climbed up into that time feels different now. I see now what I couldn't see then. Now, as then, I help the Rabbi of Shilev up, shielding his skull from the kapo's club. But now the rabbi is light as a feather. I have the feeling now that I could lift up this whole truck together with all the skeletons in it, myself included. Suddenly I know what no one else around me knows and I cry out: "Rabbi, why?"

"Because it was so decreed."

"Rabbi, who decreed? Who decreed, Rabbi?"

"Ask God."

I lift my eyes to the Auschwitz skies. Suspended against the horizon is the vision of the *shivitti*;[3] like the one usually hung framed in the front of the eyes of the prayer-leader in the synagogue. But the *shivitti* of our synagogue looks quite different here, against the sky of Auschwitz. Here it is aflame, like a torch, the glowing colors of the rainbow. But—and this is what is so extraordinary about it—its light shines only inward and upward. Auschwitz and its skies are as if they never existed, while the *shivitti* fills the whole horizon from earth to heaven.

The awe of it is upon me. I stand in the truck, one in a mass of skeletons; stand there and stare at the letters YHWH[4] glowing from within the *shivitti;* an otherworldly light. Then I stare at the twin lions, one to the left, one to the right, keeping watch between them over the secret combination: "I have set the Lord always before me." Here the lions' faces are human, and their wings are

---

[3] *shivitti:* the eighth verse from the sixteenth Psalm, "I have set the Lord always before me."

[4] YHWH: (Heb.) the explicit name of God, not to be said aloud.

spread, and the letters YHWH intertwine writhing one into the other, while I cry out: "God! God! Who decreed?! Who decreed?! God! God! Auschwitz—whose is it?"
I tremble as I lift my eyes to see the face of God in his initials, YHWH; but what I see instead is the face of the S.S. man, standing below the tailgate of the truck. Unfinished sleep is still on his face. This dawn is cold, and he keeps both hands in the pockets of his black greatcoat. He stands there watching the noiseless flow of a river of skeletons from the open gate of the barracks to the open maw of the truck. And his mouth opens wide in a long yawn.
The same S.S. man, the same yawn, the same dawn—now, just like then—when I climbed up onto the same truck. Only now I also see the *shivitti,* which I did not see then, and I call out: "God, who created Auschwitz?"
And I am in the rolling truck, one naked skeleton, amid a mass of naked skeletons, carted off to the crematorium under the watchful eye of a yawning German. Staring at him and his yawn I suddenly ask myself: Does he hate me? He doesn't even know me. He doesn't even know my name. Still staring at him I ask myself: Do I hate him? I don't even know his name, just as I don't know the names of the rest of us now being delivered to the crematorium. All I know about this German is that on a cold morning like this he'd certainly prefer snuggling under the covers of his warm bed without having to get up this early because of some load that has to leave for the crematorium.

11

All at once an additional horror seizes me, one I've not yet known: if this is so, then he could have been standing here in my place, a naked skeleton in this truck, while I, I could have been standing there instead of him, on just such a cold morning doing my job delivering him and millions like him to the crematorium—and like him I, too, would yawn, because like him I'd certainly prefer snuggling under the covers of my warm bed on a cold morning like this.

And would he watch me from within that moving truck, as I am watching him now? And would he, the musselman, think about me, the S.S. man, as I am thinking about him?

Oh Lord, merciful and compassionate Lord, am I the one, the one who's created Auschwitz? It's much worse than that he— the German facing me with the death's skull insignia on his cap, his hands deep in the pockets of his black S.S. coat—could have been in my place. It's that I—and this is the paralyzing horror—I could have been there in his place!

Oh Lord, Lord of Auschwitz heavens, illumine my ignorance of your handiwork, so that I might know who is the being within me now delivered to the crematorium–and why? And who is the being within him delivering me to the crematorium–and why? For you know that at this moment of two of us, dispatcher and dispatched, are equal sons of man, both created by you, in your image.

The truck passes through the gate of Auschwitz, above which are the German words:

Arbeit Macht Frei[5]
and I see them transmuted into the
Hebrew words
"In the image of God he created him.
I can still see: S.S. man yawning; truck in
motion; the *shivitti's* color aglow; Auschwitz
skies enflamed; and the German's face
framed against the backdrop of the letters
YHWH. The German's head is imposed
upon the *shivitti*, which faces the flaming
Auschwitz skies. And as the truck moves on
this awesome vision accompanies me, a
vision not outside of me, but inside, behind
my eyeballs, within me.

And I wonder: How is it, under these
flame-engorged Auschwitz skies, that the
winged lions hold between them the
German's face and yawn? And I observe the
process of the awesome vision rising from
my skeleton to my eyes, so that I may view it
from the outside as it accompanies me, a
mourner by my side, all the way to the
crematorium.

The truck stops. The image freezes. And
the smokestack of the crematorium juts up
behind the truck; the smokestack of a
locomotive. Billows of spark-studded smoke-
fragments of the verse: "In the image of
God..." spew forth from the locomotive's
smokestack, a flurry of stars, and the
locomotive's voice: Fummm! Fummm! And
the German's voices:
"Rrrraus!"

And the truck's tailgate, lowered. And the
bones, pouring down. And my skeleton
fingers, like then, clawing at the side of the

---

[5] *Arbeit Macht Frei:* Work sets one free.

13

truck, so that I won't be swept out like the rest. The truck keeps emptying. And I search for the coalbin...

"Rrrraus!"

"E.D'M.A.!! E.D'M.A.!!" I cry out to *shivitti.*

"Rrrraus!!!" they cry to the skeletons.

"Rrrraus!"

"E.D'M.A.!!! E.D'M.A.!!"

Then, inside the coalbin in the now evacuated truck, I didn't know where I was. I knew nothing then. Nor did I see then the burning *shivitti*, ablaze with the name of God. Perhaps someone within my skeleton did see it all, but I saw nothing, knew nothing. That other time I did see the S.S. man's face and I saw his yawn; but then I may not have had the time to think about him and his yawn. Just as I didn't then have the time to see the *shivitti* in the Auschwitz sky, though it must have been there even then. Otherwise, to whom did I cry "E.D'M.A."? To whom? I didn't then have the time for these thoughts: I was in a truck being hauled to the crematorium; whereas now I am both here and there. Not only does my body now carry within it the bony skeleton from then, but that last flickering spark, which did not quite die out in my mind then, it too, is still in its proper place now. It is what awakens me to both the now and the then, enabling me to see my mind in back of my own eyeballs: its billions of archives, as well as the billions of files in each archive. How could I have seen any of it then, when only one last spark of those billions stubbornly kept on flickering inside?

Like then, this same last spark illumines within me now the dimly-lit locked garage, where the truck is left between loads. I crawl

out of the coalbin; out in the open, in a dark hollow, a naked skeleton black with coal-dust. Existent and nonexistent, both. And shaking. And to the truckdriver arriving the next morning to open the garage I am an apparition. Stricken with fear, he runs to his commanding officers: "There's an evil spirit, a demon in the garage!" And next, the S.S. Commander stands in the doorway shouting: "Who are you? Come out or I'll shoot!"
"I'm a human being!...A human being...A human being who wants to live!...A human being! A human being! I am a human being!!!"

Jolted by the electric shock I returned to my body and stared at Prof. Bastiaans seated in the chair by my bed.

I lay in a pool sweat. I saw Prof. Bastiaans. I could still feel the touch of his finger on my own, the touch that had catapulted my body back to earthly consciousness at the moment of danger.

Eventually Prof. Bastiaans explained this physical proximity of his during every session: so that he could watch over me, and pull me back at precisely a moment like this. "If I hadn't touched you just then," he said, "I might never have been able to bring you back. You would have remained there, lost in limbo. I must follow your floating, keep you bound to me by the slenderest string, and when you reach the very end of that string that I hold in my hand, that's exactly when I must pull you back, or else you could get lost there." But this time, more clearly than then, I heard the German commander saying: "If this one succeeded in escaping the noose, I'm not going to hang him again!"

Prof. Bastiaans rose from his chair: "You need a lot of rest now, a lot of sleep. Later, when you're feeling more rested, we'll get together and go over the recording. Here is the call button within reach. The nurses will get you anything you need. They'll change your bedding. Good night, Mr. De-Nur."

Everything I underwent during the session is back alive before me, and my mind is powerfully spotlit but not blinded. I can still hear the German commander saying:

"*Ein braver Kerl!* (a tough chap) Kapo Zeppel, take him to work!"

This meant that I could simultaneously be there, in the Auschwitz garage, and here in bed in Leiden.

"Kapo Zeppel, take him to work!" My ears rang with his words, hearing them now.

What happened to me working under Kapo Zeppel has been recorded in *Salamandra*, my first volume of testimony. But was it really I who wrote it all? And is it I who lay in this bed in Prof. Bastiaan's clinic? Am I that same being I saw in tonight's session? Was that body mine?

But these are the hands that wrote *Salamandra*, wrote it in two and a half weeks, in Italy, my body still wrapped in its Auschwitz shrouds. It was obvious that I would never make it to the land of Israel. Not only did the doctors say so, but I myself knew my days were numbered. I spoke to the Israeli soldier who was nursing me: "Quick. Get me paper and pencil. I vowed to them in Auschwitz, as I stood near their ashes behind the crematorium, that I would be their voice, that I wouldn't stop telling their story till my last breath. This I must do now, while I still can."

For almost two and a half weeks I never once left my desk. I gave the manuscript to that soldier ready to carry

16

it for me to Israel. He stood over me, eyeing its title *Salamandra*, then bending closer he said softly: "The author's name—you left it out." I shouted back at him: "The name of the author?! Those who went to the crematorium wrote this book! Go on, you write their name: K. Tzetnik.[6]" And the soldier from the land of Israel, Eliahu Goldenberg, wrote in his own hand: K. Tzetnik. This nameless name has since appeared on all my books.

I lay in bed in Prof. Bastiaans's clinic, watching images pass before me like slide projections on a screen.

"Kapo Zeppel, take him to work!"

"I am a human being!... A human being who wants to live!"

"*Ein braver Kerl!*"

"You left out your name on the manuscript..."

"The nameless ones! It's Them. Them! All those anonymous ones! Write their name: K. Tzetnik!"

A young girl from Tel-Aviv read the book and invested a year of her life searching for its author. She had decided it was up to her to infuse him with the joy of living. At that point, my home at night was a bench on Rothschild Boulevard and by day, another bench facing the sea. That girl was Nike.

What was Nike doing right now? She had probably phoned Prof. Bastiaans, and he had told her I must sleep. "A lot of rest," he said. And I see Ilya Ehrenburg in the uniform of a Red Army journalist, standing next to my bed in the military hospital in Gleiwitz with tears running down his face. Before the war I had never particularly cared for his book *The Jew, Lazik*

---

[6] K. Tzetnik: K.Z. (German pronunciation ka-tzet) are the initials of Konzentration Zenter (Concentration Camp). Every K.Z. inmate was known as "K. Tzetnik Number,"—the number itself being branded into the flesh of the left arm.

17

Roitshvanz. Standing there he looked down at me, seeing for the first time a post-Auschwitz Jew, a skeleton who had been rendered speechless, while I, too, saw my first post-Auschwitz Jew. Two Jews met. He stared at me and tears ran down his face. I too wept, but my eyes were tearless.

"If the author of the book had wanted people to know his name, he wouldn't have published it anonymously," they told Nike at the publishing house. How could I explain that I didn't write the book; those who went to the crematorium nameless, they wrote it. Numbers! For two years they passed through me on their way to the crematorium, leaving me behind. Two long years, I wrote that book in two and a half weeks and then added in the preface: "Death stands waiting on the other side of my desk. In our race against time I'm still ahead. I'll finish what I can."

Should I take a sleeping pill? "Here's the call button within reach. The nurses will get you anything you need," the professor had said. On the road from Auschwitz I went back to the ghetto where I had hidden my sister Daniella's diary[7]. White snow covered the ghetto. Death was silent in the white ghetto. The snow hid everything. The snow will hide Auschwitz too, and no one will know what happened here.

I then went back to Auschwitz, still wearing the camp shrouds. The iron doors to the crematorium oven gaped wide open, now cold, the dark meeting my eye. The long shovel of iron that had delivered human beings to the fire stood leaning against the oven's maw, like a baker's shovel. The blocks were empty, silent. The brick stove too was silent, running down the center of the block from one gate to the other. At one time, when

---

[7] See *House of Dolls.*

camp blocks such as this had been a stable, the stoves had been well-fueled. As the place became Auschwitz the brick stove became an indoor execution spot: over it, faces down, inmates were flogged to death. I stood inside the block that had so recently housed me, one inmate out of that thousand. I inched closer to my old hutch. It was both vacant and full. Here "Baby" lay at my side. His weird way of dying, even in Auschwitz, had been a novelty. Here lay Vevke the cobbler whom Franzl had killed on top of the brick stove with twenty-five strokes. Here, on these planks, lay the Rabbi of Shilev, whom I had helped up onto the truck that carried us to the crematorium. They and the others are buried within me, and each continues living his own life within me. Over their ashes I vowed to be a voice to them, and when I left Auschwitz they walked with me, they and the soundless Auschwitz blocks, the soundless crematorium, the soundless horizons, and at the front the mountain of ash to show me the way.

"Nurse! Nurse!" I pressed the button. "If my wife calls to inquire, please tell her I'm not sleeping, and that if she feels up to it she can come."

"Look around you. See what you are getting into. You don't belong here," I said to Nike after she finally located me in my Tel-Aviv cellar and asked me to marry her. "Go back to your own life, and don't look back. I don't want you to be harmed. Here, lungs breathe gas chamber fumes. Here, love cries out at night from the throats of the crematorium chimneys. Here, the wind carries the ashes of cremated legs, once long and beautiful as yours; ashes of a body like yours, lithe and in full bloom; the ashes of a face like your own, and lips like your lips. Only the gaze of those eyes, like the gleam in yours, hovers here unconsumed. How will you inhale this air?"

"Mr. De-Nur, you have to get some sleep!" the nurse scolded me. "No more of this 'my wife' business. Just rest! Take this with plenty of water, Mr. De-Nur, and get some rest. Those are the professor's instructions. Sleep well, Mr. De-Nur." And she left the room.

"No more of this 'my wife' business!" I married Nike in my tiny cellar. She left her parents' ten-room apartment for my basement and came to share my existence.

"If you want to help yourself—and I believe you do—you'll need to cooperate."

Prof. Bastiaans addressed me gently. We sat in a small anteroom, not where he interviewed his patients, nor where he treated them. I felt like a troublemaker, but it gave me no pleasure. In fact it revolted me, but I had no choice. I was incapable of providing answers. Questions, usually, were anathema; a trauma rooted in the torture cellar of the Gestapo in Katowice. In my mind I rebuked the Professor seated opposite me: I made my conditions clear to you from the beginning. They were my opening statement upon meeting you. Perhaps I didn't use normal everyday language, but at the time I was convinced you had thoroughly understood me. Even now I believe that you knew what I intended though I may have used code. What other way could those words have been understood: "You will open the gate for me, let me go through, while you remain outside." And what else could be the meaning of, "You remain outside?"

"Prof. Bastiaans," I say, "I honestly want to help myself. It's why I came to you. I only wish I knew how to do it."

"The 'how' is also part of the treatment. I have read your books, I am aware how qualified you are in analyzing emotional states and in precisely describing them. I obviously didn't see what you saw. During our sessions all I heard you say was 'Why?' over and over. Whom did you direct your question to? What did you see? Who was it you saw?"

I was distraught. It had been a whole week now that I had been wandering in the woods around the clinic encapsulated in chaos. The LSD session had left me frightened, stunned. I had never imagined facing the situation I was in now. Moreover, I realized that, had I been anyone else, another patient behaving in this fashion, Prof. Bastiaans would have sent me packing. The tone of reverence with which his patients pronounced his name was by now a common phenomenon, as was the awe they felt preparing for their sessions with him. I felt sad seeing him sit across from me, addressing me so tamely, even tenderly, like a mother dealing with an obnoxious child when all she'd truly like to do is give him a good slap. This man, to whom people came flocking from all over the world, uncomplainingly awaiting their sessions with him, Prof. Bastiaans, now sat across from me, asking that I be good enough to help myself by cooperating with him, by relating to him what it was I'd witnessed under LSD, whom it was I had seen, to whom my agonized question "Why?" had been repeatedly raised and—"I am a human being!"—what did this cry mean? But how to relate to him all of these things? An entire week since the session, and my own mind had not yet absorbed the fearsome vision. I shut my eyes and made an effort to cooperate.

"I saw the *shivitti*...and I saw God in a cloud...God's spirit hovering in the letters of his name...his glory filled the horizon, from the Auschwitz earth to the Auschwitz skies...and the face of an S.S. man and his yawn...and the vortex of the letters YHWH. There was a tangle of snakes squirming at the center of the *shivitti*. And I was anxious to see the face of Satan, creator of Auschwitz, but instead I suddenly saw my own face imposed over the frenzied snakes ... on my head an S.S. cap, the death skull emblem above the visor and through the empty eyesockets of that death skull, I watched the truck driving toward the crematorium and I yawned and yawned and kept looking at that S.S. man, now just one more naked skeleton, amid a mass of naked skeletons being hauled off to the burning—"

So I talked on and on, with my eyes shut. And when I finally looked outside myself, there was Prof. Bastiaans's bronzed face. I fell silent. His green-blue eyes went on staring at me.

"Prof. Bastiaans," I said, "Perhaps this meeting is premature, too soon after the session?"

"Oh definitely," he blurted out as if to himself, "You need a lot of rest, Mr. De-Nur. A lot of rest."

He rose somewhat heavily, uttering not a word about the time of the next session. He inserted the tape recorder into his briefcase. The odd meeting was apparently at its end. I offered him my hand on my way out of the little anteroom.

Outside Nike was waiting for me. Eager as she was to know what had transpired at my first tape-deciphering session with the professor, she still didn't ask a single question.

"He asked me questions," I said.

There was enough in that statement to arouse Nike's concern. She was only too familiar with what I went through when confronted with personal questions. At the Eichmann trial in Jerusalem, had the judge not asked me personal questions, I might not have been rushed to the hospital with my face half-twisted in paralysis. Now Nike raised frightened eyes to me while I hastened to calm her: "Nothing happened. You can see I came out of it in one piece. That first LSD session must have worked a miracle if I could so miraculously come up with answers to Prof. Bastiaans's questions."

Nike's face lit up. "In that case, I have good news for you," she said. "I found us an apartment. Now you can be at home and go for treatment at the same time. It's in Noordwijk-on-Sea. A fabulous apartment! It's a tourist area, with all the amenities."

In Noordwijk the tourist season was at its peak. Most of the tourists were from Germany. I loved swimming in the sea and lying on the warm sand, soaking up the sun. "Rest, Mr. De-Nur, a lot of rest!" A welcome instruction from my doctor which I gladly followed until the day Prof. Bastiaans's secretary phoned to inform me that the forth-coming session was scheduled for the day after next.

I lay on the sandy beach, haunted by crazy thoughts about how, when I was on the LSD again, I could avoid a head-on confrontation with the real issue that had brought me here. This particular issue so terrified me that at times I felt ready to jump up and bolt for home. I was like a man slated for surgery whose chief surgeon is not too sure the patient will make it through the operation. These thoughts drained me. Sometimes I managed to push them aside, shake them off. I kept the same safe distance between me and my thoughts that a careful driver does between his car and the car in front of him. But the secretary's morning phone call, the appointment of day and hour, forced me to prepare for the meeting between myself and the danger within me: the hidden enemy.

Nike's days were busy. Her arrival in Holland from California was her spontaneous response to my unexpected transatlantic news: "I'm going to Leiden!" Nike was absorbed in her divinity studies while I absorbed Noordwijk's sea, sun, and glistening mass of outstretched tourist bodies surrounding me. I felt like a condemned man with two days left until his execution. And amid all this, I noticed a group of happy young German tourists, their chests and arms bizarrely tatooed. In amused fascination they stared at the ordinary, no-frills number they discovered on my forearm. To them, the straightforward blue number was a novelty and they seemed to be absorbed in reading meaning into it. Finally one of them approached me.

The blood pounded in my veins. This was the very first time that I had exposed the number on my arm. For the thirty years since it was burned into my flesh I had been very careful to keep it covered from strange eyes. I had not had a short-sleeved shirt in my closet for thirty years. In my country, during the long, sun-scorched

25

summers, I preferred to endure mortification of the flesh, sweating in my long-sleeved shirts. The toughest places were the public swimming pools where I invariably draped a towel over my left arm as I walked. At the pool I was certain that all eyes were focused on my left arm. And all this subterfuge because I had never learned to live with these six digits branded in my flesh and soul. To this day I cannot recall the digits by heart. To get my number right, I need to look at my arm. In fact, because of this trauma, my mind cannot retain numbers.

Only in Noordwijk, on its sand, did I first uncover the number to the sun. Perhaps I could there because no one knew me. It wasn't Israel, where every schoolchild knows the meaning of a plain blue number on someone's arm, knows where that person has been. I know I didn't conceal the number out of shame or guilt. Not at all. Then why? Only Satan of Auschwitz knows. And there in Noordwijk, where my mind was preparing to be free from the curse over my life, there was a German, of all people, standing over me, staring at the number on my arm and mumbling something. I didn't hear him, didn't register what was around me. Any minute something horrible would happen, I knew. A crazy beast was rearing awake within me ready to plunge its fangs into the throat of this being standing over me. I jumped to my feet, spewing curses, and ran. I leaped over basking bodies and then up to Astrid Boulevard. I had run that way before through the ghetto streets when I first stole out of my house into the street with my yellow Jew-star sewn to my coat next to my heart. At that moment it seemed certain to me that everyone, from every house, from every window, from every direction, even from every cobblestone, pointed at me with their fingers and hissed: "Branded! He's branded! Branded!" and then I broke into a gallop and scurried home.

My eyes are still imprinted with the smiling face of that young German who found the tattoo on my arm to be so plain and therefore unique; and I ask myself if our period in Germany history will impress future generations as a plain, therefore unique tattoo.

GATE TWO

That in that day he that escapeth
shall come unto thee,
to cause thee, to hear it with thine ears.

EZEKIEL 24:26

GATE TWO

(Prof. Bastiaans recording:)
LSD treatment of Mr. De-Nur,
Session Two,
at my clinic,
Psychiatric Department,
State University, Leiden.

I lay in the same room, in the same bed, seized by the same trembling. I had asked for this room. And in my heart I murmured a silent prayer that once I was under the influence of LSD I would again manage to avoid the sight of that which I had come here to see.

I was fully aware of the reason I was lying there in the bed, but my natural instinct for self-preservation suggested a few test flights before setting off for my destination. I was like one perched on the brink of a chasm, forced to leap to the other side.

Prof. Bastiaans turned away from the recorder and seated himself in the chair by my bed. The chemical was in his hand. He was ready.

In Auschwitz, whenever death closed in on me, the sum of my preceding life passed before my eyes. What came to me now while Prof. Bastiaans readied the syringe was the totality of my Auschwitz years. I stood facing the Auschwitz gate. To enter there was why I had come. To stand in supplication: if I'm doomed to re-enter, may I be granted, this session also, to go no further than the outer corridors of hell; let me once again grow gradually accustomed to the inferno. My first

31

experience had taught me that before the LSD took over my mind, I had the power to program the direction I wanted the session to take me.

"Relax, Mr. De-Nur, relax."

I was amazed that he had noticed my inner trembling from where he sat. I was relieved he hadn't yet instructed me to turn toward the wall so he could jab me with the needle.

"I hear something happened to you in Noordwijk," he said. "Your wife sounded very worried on the phone. Are you ready to tell me about it?"

The scream almost erupted from my mouth: "Not now! Not now!" The moment the young German bent over me with his smiling face as I lay there in the Noordwijk sand, his was the face of Siegfried, the S.S. man, dragging me by the feet all that endless distance from the S.S. living quarters back to the block after I saw my branded sister. He hurled me to the floor and then paused for a moment to stare down at me, checking if I was still alive.

"With your permission, Prof. Bastiaans, not now, not before the shot!"

"That's the point, Mr. De-Nur, before the shot," Prof. Bastiaans said this as if he had heard my objections before. "In my opinion the timing is right. It's been thirty years since the Holocaust, and I know how things have a way of slipping into the past, though they continue their existence in us as trauma in its various manifestations. The proof lies in your coming here, Mr. De-Nur, thirty years after the events. There is no doubt that these events have a life of their own, only they have left the surface of memory for the depths of the subconscious. Our task is to raise these events from the subconscious so we can see and treat them. I'm afraid you are not too helpful, Mr. De-Nur, by resisting cooperation. This substance which I am about to transmit to a certain area of your brain, will evoke images and situations that can be compared to hieroglyphs. To decipher them we must look at them; study them. These hieroglyphs won't be sent to me, Mr. De-Nur, but to you. And if you leave me out of this, how can I do the decoding? And now for the main point—and this you must realize—the LSD won't work by itself. It needs your cooperation to raise the events from subconscious to memory and from memory to vision and from vision to speech. Well then, if you so recently had a shock, it is my opinion that now is the best time to deal with it, while you can still see it, while the experience is fresh enough to pull it out like the poisoned thorn it is, before it works its way into the fabric of your soul. And you do want this. This essentially is what your trembling body is broadcasting to you."

"Very much so, Prof. Bastiaans," I say. "I fully appreciate your efforts to put me at ease, free to express myself. Believe me, I would very much like to follow your guidance. This is what I came to Leiden for—to save myself. But what can I do when I'm struck mute? I have neither word nor name for it all. Genesis says: 'And Adam gave names ...'. When God finished creating the earth and everything upon it, Adam was asked to give names to all that God had created. Till 1942 there was no Auschwitz in existence. For Auschwitz there is no name other than Auschwitz. My heart will be ripped to pieces if I say, 'In Auschwitz they burned people alive!' or 'In Auschwitz people died of starvation.' But that is not Auschwitz. People have died of starvation before, and people did burn alive before. But that is not Auschwitz. What, then, is Auschwitz? I don't have the word to express it; I don't have the name for it. Auschwitz is a primal phenomenon. I have no key to unlock it. But don't the tears of the mute speak his anguish? And don't his screams cry his distress? Don't his bulging eyes reveal the horror? I am that mute.

"When the prosecutor invited me to speak at the Eichmann trial, I begged him to forego my testimony. The prosecutor then said to me: 'Mr. De-Nur, this is a trial whose protocol depends on testimony to prove there was a place called Auschwitz and a description of what happened there.' The mere hearing of those words sickened me, and I said: 'Sir, describing Auschwitz is beyond me!' Hearing me, his staff eyed me with suspicion. 'You, the person who wrote those books, you expect us to believe you can't explain to the judges what Auschwitz was?' I fell silent. How could I communicate to them the way I myself burn, searching for the word to name the look in the eyes of those who would walk through me to the crematorium, with eyes that fused with mine? The prosecutor was not convinced and I appeared at the Eichmann trial. Then came the judges' first question about Auschwitz, and no sooner did I squeeze out a few miserable sentences than I dropped to the floor half-paralyzed, face distorted, and was rushed to the hospital. Now have I made myself clear, Prof. Bastiaans?"

"This is exactly what I wanted to hear from you, Mr. De-Nur. Your incapacity to give words to your experiences is at the root of your soul's torment. Just allow the words to flow so we can both see what your eyes witnessed. If right now you harness your mind to this task, then quite possibly this chemical in my hand may help you. This is the purpose of our having this conversation: to direct your thinking to what's presently blocking the passageways of your soul.

34

"Indeed," he said, drawing closer with the syringe, "the more refined a man's senses, the sharper he is, the better his aim on the target. Moreover, he's equally as quick at deflecting the searchlight from the things he's out to hide. That's why, when I earlier brought up the episode in Noordwijk—"

And suddenly_____

I am marching in the procession. I watch myself from a distance. The Gestapo has granted the Jews one hour to vacate the Jewish Quarter and move into the ghetto. Black uniforms go from house to house shooting dawdlers. I am part of the procession that I watch. The procession is frozen, petrified like a motion picture stopped in mid-frame on the screen.

I see myself a detail in the procession. Given no more than one hour, everyone has grabbed whatever came to hand. Vevke the cobbler marches ahead of me, his workbench on his back, his head drooping, like the head of a horse pulling a heavily-laden dray. I myself hadn't made it to the violin case when the shooting began; this is why I'm carrying my violin in my arms, bared. Vevke, head lowered, downcast eyes shooting sideways glances to those flanking him, mutters: "Jews, don't weep! Don't give these hangmen the satisfaction. Jews, put your faith in God!"

The horizon breaks up into all the colors and the procession reflects those colors. I walk in back of Vevke, my eyes riveted on his cobbler's bench which changes from blinding yellow-green to ultraviolet, and transforms from one shape to another. The procession is totally frozen, static, but Vevke's cobbler's bench is perpetually moving. Bit by bit, my eyes watching, the bench pours itself from Vevke's shoulders, elongating like that clock of Salvador Dali's which spills from the table's edge to the ground. While Vevke holds onto the bench, with both hands spread left and right, his palms appearing nailed to the wood which bit by bit becomes a cross, aflame with infrared rays, incandescent. So Vevke drags along with his cross in this procession of the Jews. To the ghetto. Once upon a time the city's dump.

"Don't weep, Jews, don't weep! Don't give the hangmen the satisfaction!" And every which-way Vevke twists his head I catch a glimpse of his face in its nonstop transmutation. For one moment he has the face of Reb Nachman the Bretzlaver, causing a voice from heaven to thunder down: "Make way for the Messiah, Son of Joseph, make way!" Another moment his face is the Rabbi of Shilev's, the way I saw him locked in the isolation block just before our transport was sent to the crematorium. And concurrent with his facial meta-morphoses are the color changes of the procession which marches forward while it stays put. Static, it is suspended cloudlike in the sky. The sky rains down the letters of the scriptural verse: "Like the Son of Man come with the clouds of heaven..." I read the words vertical as Chinese script descending onto the petrified procession, whose center is Vevke nailed to his shouldered cobbler's bench, one moment Dali's clock; another Jacob's ladder with angels going up and down; or another moment, a cross. Great awe befalls me. The procession freezes and I am the breath in mid-asphyxiation of the immobile, marching mass. And locked in this no-exit stranglehold, I must breathe while we proceed to the ghetto, of late the city's dump. "Air. Air..." I rasp.

"**What do you see, Mr. De-Nur? Tell me, Mr. De-Nur!**" The voice reaches me like thunder rolling down from the distant skies, so distant. "What — do — you — see ... see ... see?"

I see Vevke's cobbler's bench change into an altar. I see the Old Man of Shpuleh[8] in the High Priest's vestments and I see the face of Vevke, now the Bretzlaver Rabbi. He stands in the city's garbage dump, now ghetto, the altar borne on his back, the voice thundering as if from on high: "Messiah, Son of Joseph—make way!" And the Old Man of Shpuleh in the High Priest's vestments calls out to him in Arabic: "Mahrum! Mahrum!"[9]

And I ask my soul: Are we—the procession, with Vevke shouldering his cobbler's bench—doomed to stay frozen together like this forever, like a petrified parade at the heart of the garbage dump ghetto? Now I see Vevke bound to the brick stove in Franzl's barracks at Auschwitz. I can't see his face because he's arched over the brick stove, head down, arms stretched to his right and left, each hand bound to an iron hook—crucified. His pants, dropped,

---

[8] The Old Man of Shpuleh: nineteenth-century Hasidic-Polish rabbi, master and initiator of Reb Nahman the Bretzlaver's unique Hasidic teachings and, later, by inherent authority, his excommunicator.

[9] *mahrum:* outcast.

cover his bare feet. Terror seizes me. Block Chief Franzl has brought Vevke to the Akeda.[10] The sacrifice is ready.

"Mr. De-Nur, what do you see . . . see . . . see?"

The voice searching for me rises from a deep pit. I see Vevke's two naked buttocks casting white fire into every nook of the dark block. A thousand inmates catch their breath. Any moment now Franzl will step out of his cubicle, the pure-white cane in his hand, and he will count off twenty-five strokes, one by one, onto Vevke's withered buttocks. The sacrifice is ready.

This is the cane Franzl had removed at the unloading platform from a blind man's hand as he came tumbling into Auschwitz out of the packed cattle cars. Franzl, like a woodchopper raising his axe to split a log, lifts this cane. And every time the cane crashes into Vevke's naked buttocks salvos of sparks in all colors of the rainbow come spewing out, glowing stars bursting like fireworks and dispersing throughout the darkness of the block. Soon the orderlies will remove Vevke's carcass to toss it onto the pile of corpses behind the building, the ones awaiting the rounds of the corpse commando, who will load them onto their pushcarts and deliver them to their destined burning. Never yet has the life breath remained in a mussulman's body after the twenty-five strokes of the barracks chief's white cane. An unbreakable cane. What

---

[10] Akeda: the binding of Isaac when he was being prepared for the sacrifice.

38

would a blind man want with a cane, Franzl had quipped—his truck knows its way to the crematorium. Suddenly darkness in the block. Vevke is unbound by orderlies and removed to the pile of corpses and all the lights go out. Vevke will soon become ash. I see smoke rising out of the crematorium chimney, coils of smoke, interspersed with sparks. I stand and stare, expecting to see Vevke the cobbler within rising smoke. Day and night, night and day, the smoke rises ceaselessly from the chimneys of the crematorium. "Rabbi! Rabbi!" I cry out. "Is it possible that this smoke goes up to heaven and just vanishes there?"

"What do you see, Mr. De-Nur? Tell us—what do you see?"

I see millions of sparks, shooting out of the smokestack, as from a pipe inserted into the core of the oven below, a kind of mysterious flaming laboratory. I see one and one-half million children, millions of young girls in the bloom of innocence, millions of mothers whose young breasts are full with milk, millions of youths in their prime, millions of aged men and women—and all of them cast like coal into the fiery maw, to feed the core of the oven in the mystery lab of Auschwitz.

"Rabbi! Rabbi! What is manufactured in this oven whose flames are fed by millions of bodies? Endlessly, endlessly. What is the product of this factory?"

"Rabbi! Rabbi! I see the ashes from the bodies, but what about the souls of millions

39

who passed like heavy water into the furnace—what do they produce? Rabbi! What will be the end product manufactured from the souls of one and one-half million burnt children?"

Around me is day. Around me is night. For weeks. For years. My hand feels the moment fracture. I see the color and the light of the fracture. I see Time. I have the power to draw it: face and form. I taste Time, chew it, swallow it. Time is inside me. I can see it though I know Time is faceless, so I snap its picture for a keepsake: It is engraved on the pupils of my eyes. Time is within me, I am Time, and, as Time's stand-in, I stand in Auschwitz, between Block 14 and the roll call area, my eyes watching the ascent of this crematorium smoke, waiting to catch sight of Vevke the cobbler, who's supposed to be in these twists of smoke. With my own eyes I witnessed the corpse commando arrive to toss him on their pushcart; with my own eyes I witnessed how their pushcart became a cobbler's bench, and the cobbler's bench become an altar; an altar whose likeness was fashioned as divinely as God prescribed to Moses in the Torah. Furthermore, the altar of Auschwitz shines with more radiance than the biblical altar.

Once the orderlies tossed Vevke on top of the corpse pile behind the block, I came out to touch the white fire emanating from his body. I wanted that fire to brand my hand with its stigma. This may allow me the grace of sharing his lot. Vevke is greater than Isaac, who got away from that altar. But no angel materialized in the Auschwitz barracks to stay the white cane in Franzl's hand. It

was his white fire I wanted to touch. I didn't
know if I would be graced with such a fire
when it was my turn with the corpse detail's
pushcart. I witness how Vevke's skeleton is
tossed, a burnt offering, on the altar. My ears
echo with verses from heaven: "and take an
unblemished lamb...and sacrifice it."[11] "And I
will judge between lamb and lamb."[12] Now I
expect to see Vevke ascend with the smoke,
and I stand and stare, and I am Time, and
just as Time is at a standstill in Auschwitz, I
too am at a standstill in Auschwitz. And I
stand and I watch and I witness:

No, it's not Vevke ascending from the
crematorium smoke, but he himself, none
other, Ashmadai,[13] King of Hades, to his
right Shamhazai, to his left Azael,[14] as I
came to know them through the Book of
Enoch the Negro. I shake with terror. I
scream. I want to hide my face, to be
unseen. It's because of the fiery
kaleidoscope blinding my eyes. In Auschwitz
there is nowhere to run, no place to hide.

**"Tell us, Mr. De-Nur, what's frightening you?" The
voice comes reaching for me from every corner of
Auschwitz. "What is frightening . . . frightening . . .
frightening?"**

Auschwitz is a flaming pyre. I know I
have been summoned to witness the fire-
belching sight. Ashmadai, King of Auschwitz.
Here he is. I see him with my own eyes
emerging from the furnace in his ascent from

---

[11] Exod. 12:5
[12] Ezek. 34:22
[13] Ashmadai: Satan's name.
[14] Shamhazai, Azael: servant-angels to Ashmadai.

41

the chimney, from the hidden holies of his abode. Cloaked by the smoke, he wafts to the heights of heaven, with Shamhazai and Azael unfurling a canopy over his head. Mushroom-like, the specter looms in the sky: Shamhazai and Azael are about to anoint Ashmadai as the new King of Kings, lord of the universe. With blaring trumpets they declare to the four corners of the earth that the new name of this sovereign of the universe will no longer be Ashmadai, but Nucleus! His birthplace: The heart of the furnace in the mystery laboratory, Auschwitz. Manufactured from a new substance, altogether unique, Nucleus is the concentrate of the souls of one and one-half million living, breathing children.

I lift my eyes to the skies of Auschwitz and I see Nucleus on his throne, under his majestic mushroom dome. And the dome outgrows Auschwitz, his birthplace, and is borne to the four directions of the celestial compass, till it has completely blotted out the sun and the firmament.

I am shaken by the terror of utter darkness. A voice calls: "You, Son of Man, eat this scroll!" and I cry and cry: "God, why? Why?"

I turn away to avoid the looming specter and on the horizon I see the *shivitti*, hanging there opposite me, and, at its hub, the letters of the holy name YHWH, squirming like a tangle of vipers, and, imposed on it, my face, the S.S. cap on my head. *Shivitti* changes like a digital watch that alternates date and hour. Opposite the mushroom of Nucleus the letters of the name of God catch fire; but as the Hebrew letters change into the tangle of vipers with my face in the S.S. cap superimposed on it, then *shivitti* goes into hiding, and Nucleus the King wins the upper hand. I raise my voice, shouting across to my own face hiding the *shivitti:* "Oh God, God! It was Vevke the cobbler I asked to see in the smoke, not Satan! God, oh God! In your war with Satan don't turn your face from me! Don't surrender me to Franzl's white cane! My God, my God, don't forsake me!"

"What do you see, Mr. De-Nur? What hurts? What—do—you—see?"

Oh, Lord, let me survive. Let me hold out... hold out. I took an oath, I made a vow to be their voice. Spare me, Lord, spare me! No one here will be left alive. Oh, God, I'll be witness to your fulgent presence in the letters of your name! I'll be witness to your face in Auschwitz, Lord! Lord!

An electric jolt, and I was tossed back into my body, in bed. I opened my eyes. Prof. Bastiaans was seated in the chair by my bed, while next to my head was the unfamiliar face of a stranger, squatting. I was soaked in tears and perspiration. I heard: "What did you see, Mr. De-Nur? What are you still seeing? What images keep surfacing in you?"

The man whose face was next to my head asked me these questions. His voice sounded familiar, although I had never seen him before. His questions dived into my inner ear as if I had heard them in a previous incarnation. I was enraged at Prof. Bastiaans: Why did he invite a stranger to invade my privacy without first asking my permission? I stared at the face of the man who was vexing me so.

43

I said nothing. I was like someone returned from another world. The stranger rose to his feet and Prof. Bastiaans saw him out.

After a while, when I had recovered, Prof. Bastiaans anticipated my question: "That was Prof. Dijkhaus of the University of Leiden. He is a theologian, an expert in his field. I was grateful he agreed to be present during your session. I needed his assistance to get an understanding of the spheres where you find yourself floating under the influence of the LSD. Together we also tried to analyze the recording. But we couldn't learn anything further. Only you can help yourself. Professor Dijkhaus tried everything he knew to encourage you to answer, but you did not cooperate with us. Not even under the influence of the LSD!"

Weeks went by and I was strangely exhausted. I still felt the last session in my bones. I was worried. Time passed, yet whenever the next session came to mind I got the shakes, which worried me all the more. If what I had experienced the last time had such an effect on me, and if it was only a corridor leading to the event that brought me to Leiden, then what would happen when I was actually in the thick of it? I was in the grip of distress. Prof. Bastiaans wouldn't send a cop to haul me off for treatment, but whenever his secretary phoned for an appointment, I panicked and asked to put it off.

At times I went to the clinic, seeking closeness with the other patients. They came from all over, all with their own tales, though I hadn't yet met any other Auschwitz survivor there. I made friends with almost all of them. And while I was idling my time away, quite a few finished and left for home. Some new arrivals were eager for my company, the veteran. I questioned each of them, anxious to hear what each felt after a session. What effect did LSD have on them? And almost unanimously they gave me the identical answer: if only they didn't have to wait so long between sessions.

In confused embarrassment I bade each one goodbye. I kicked myself: What was wrong with me? Why wasn't it the same for me? Why was I the only one labeled uncooperative by Prof. Bastiaans? He may have been right, but how did not cooperating relate to my fears? I had learned that I could program the focus of the LSD session, hadn't I? Here my mind stopped: but could

I? Did I pave the way for the experiences during that last session? And once LSD had taken over, was I still navigator of my spaceship?

At this point I determined not to quit no matter what happened. And if so, I'd better get up and go for it. Get my head together, try over and over, rehearse again and again, take my medicine, until I reached the ultimate answer.

So I went to Prof. Bastiaans's secretary to ask for the appointment. The secretary flipped through her appointment book without raising her eyes. "I see you've already cancelled three appointments, Mr. De-Nur. The earliest opening is two weeks from today."

"I'll be patient," I said, and walked out feeling good.

Making my way home I felt restored. I didn't ask myself what had changed. I didn't feel like soul-searching. I was just happy without knowing the why and the wherefore of it. Also there was the secretary's smile bathing me in its compassion. And I, I actually asked for the appointment!

Making my way home my face felt radiant, and I wanted Nike to see me. I had been reeking of wretchedness those past few weeks. During this time, the secretary informed me, Nike had called on the professor. That Nike kept their meeting secret told me the nature of their discussion. Nike must have been worried sick. Up till then she had not heard a word from me to explain my state, nor had she asked. Had she asked, would I have had an answer? Could I have told her that I was still stuck in the last session? That I was still there, inside? I could only imagine how far Nike's concern must have taken control, for her to have spoken privately with Prof. Bastiaans! Now it was clear she was behind the secretary's three phone calls for an appointment. I had asked other patients wise in the ways of the clinic how they went about canceling an appointment when the need arose. My question itself threw them. Each one of them felt that canceling an appointment would be like phoning the Messiah and telling him to put his Coming on hold.

Each one gave the same answer, and I left with my ears ringing with Nike's oft-repeated decree: "Face it, my man, you're different." No way. I had never accepted that designation. But that day, a day different from all other days, I finally let the question in: What if Nike was right? It takes a friend to be this honest. A stranger would turn his back on an oddball like me. Didn't Prof. Bastiaans keep saying the same thing as Nike? He, of course, used professional jargon, but the message was the same. And what do you say? The inner voice zeroed in on me: Are you going to say you're like all the rest of them in the clinic? Nobody's listening. This is just between the two of us. Aren't you finally ready to confess you're different?

I hadn't any idea what the others went through after LSD shot them into orbit; I had no idea what they saw or what they came away with from their journey. I, for one, floated in limbo for weeks before I could re-enter the atmosphere to make a soft landing. Did that make me strange? Or could the difference simply be that they originated from all kinds of other German camps, while I was the only one from Auschwitz? Or could the difference be accounted for by the fact that most of the others were not Jews?

The door to Nike's room stood open. I watched her immersed in her work. I dared not get close and disturb her.

Jauntily I went off for a stroll along Astrid Boulevard. It felt so good to walk Noordwijk's narrow alleys. Still, my favorite path led through the streets of the ancient university town of Leiden. I have a soft spot for the Dutch, an affection rooted in Auschwitz, where we all were what we were. And there is no need to elaborate on what we were like in Auschwitz. Still, I can never forget the first time I met Dutch Jews there. The faces of two of them have been with me since. One was nicknamed "Baby" at Auschwitz. The other's name remains unknown to me. However, I will never forget the rebellion contorting his face when he refused to execute the German's order. He and I, standing over a pit, were among the labor crew.[15] The crematorium was stuffed beyond capacity. All at once more trucks arrived from the train platform carrying a living load of gypsy women and children. Since the crematorium could not cope with any more and the holding barracks were filled beyond maximum capacity, the trucks dumped their load into the pit, and the S.S. man turned to address the first man in our row and ordered him to take the container of kerosene and empty it over the women and children.

"No! No!" he said in Dutch.

I'll never forget the anguished look of refusal on his face; just as my ears will keep resounding with his Dutch "No!" A "No" of that kind had never before been given to a German in Auschwitz.

While the women and children were beginning to catch fire the S.S. man walked over behind our row and kicked the Dutchman in the buttocks. The latter's skeleton-body, like a piece of driftwood, toppled into the flames.

"*Kan niet lopen.*"[16] When we were marched off to the work site, the Dutchman, his step unsure, had limped by my side. "*Kan niet lopen*" he had mumbled, and it was then I had my first experience with Dutch. Looking

---

[15] Members of the labor crew worked until they dropped dead.
[16] "*Kan niet lopen*": "I can't walk."

48

at him, I understood the foreign words. Since his "No" to the S.S. man and his flight into the fire, I have not been able to get "*Kan niet lopen*," syllable for syllable, out of the mind.

Can you appreciate the simple humanity, the sheer ordinariness of those three words uttered while being marched in Auschwitz accompanied by S.S. hounds? It was as if you were relaxing in an easy chair in your living room, watching TV and complaining: I'm pooped. Now, for the contortion. Picture yourself leaving for work in the morning and suddenly right outside your home you come across a huge pit filled with women and children. Someone then hands you a container of kerosene and tells you to empty it over their heads to reduce them to ashes. Can you imagine the convulsion that would rip your face to pieces? That was the convulsion on the face of that Jew from Holland standing not too far from the crematorium in Auschwitz, he who said "No!" to a German with a stunned look on his skeleton-face, he who, limping along beside me escorted by S.S. and their hounds, could also say, "*Kan niet lopen.*"

The second Dutchman was "Baby," co-occupant of the planks of my hutch—in Rotterdam the Director-General of a major shipping company and in Auschwitz the apple of the block chief's eye. The man had a special power: by screwing up his face and winking with the slits that were left of his kindly eyes, he ignited an irresistible impulse for laughter in the block chief, that omnipotent dealer of life and death to a thousand inmates. He was the one to dub this Dutch Jew "Baby." Baby, the chief's chosen clown, strutted around on two Chaplinesque feet, his shoulders a grotesque slope, his head and neck a mass of encrustations, so that the crown looked like it was topped by an elongated skullcap. Just

49

for the hell of it the chief would occasionally allow Baby to lick the bottom of the barrel once the soup was distributed. Baby would plunge his head and arms into the barrel, leaving only his Chaplinesque feet visible. One thousand prisoners ogled him with envy. On emerging—one single mass of filth—from the barrel, Baby's tumorous skull would be indistinguishable from his face. He would then flash his wonder-wink and make the orderlies laugh because the chief was laughing.

One night, as he lay by my side on the planks, I saw an endless stream of tears pouring down his scab-covered cheeks and into his encrusted ears.

"What is it, Baby?"

And he—immobile, staring ahead, his hands cradling his head in shame, brought out these words:

"You see me only as the clown, don't you? But do you know what's in my head? If it weren't for the clown they'd have thrown me into the oven long ago. Perhaps I'd be better off in the oven, but then what'll happen to my Zizi, my love? She's counting on seeing her handsome lover again. I didn't always look like this, you know. Every single time I look at myself nowadays, it just steels my will to hold on for Zizi, Zizi who keeps constant vigil for me. By coming back to her I want to show Zizi that I outlasted Auschwitz."

And then came the big event, the day of the Auschwitz freak show. The chief, Franzl, showed off Baby, his main attraction, to the block master, who had thought of a plan for a good laugh. The inmates were all ordered to the parade ground and commanded to form a circle around Baby, who stood dead center. In an orderly's hand was the bowl containing the weekly ration of marmalade—enough for one blob of marmalade to be spread—today's the day!—on each inmate's bread ration. The block master helped himself to the jar and then dumped its entire contents over Baby's scab-covered skull. He and the chief were in stitches. *Ach, Gott,* what a circus! Then the master asked one thousand prisoners how they'd like a lick of marmalade.

Inmates all over Baby. A voracious multitude, limbs tangling, arms and legs flailing, biting and being bitten in a mass frenzy. The two German spectators were convulsed with laughter. Later, on the deserted parade ground, only a chewed carcass remained, gnawed as if by a horde of famished rats. The orderlies dragged the bleeding blob behind the barracks. And so, atop the pile of corpses, lay Zizi's dream—Zizi who kept vigil in Rotterdam for her handsome lover.

Strolling down the alleyways of Noordwijk I marched in Auschwitz, by my side the Dutchman murmuring *"Kan niet lopen."* But I had the skies of Holland over my head and the earth of Noordwijk under my feet. The faces of Dutch people moved by me— women with shopping bags in their hands, men, laborers, girls in bathing suits on their way to the beach—and I kept on marching the Auschwitz march with the nameless Dutch dawdler by my side. I looked at each face passing by, and I felt a sudden urge to say "hi" to every single one of them. I couldn't hold it back any longer. I said to the woman walking towards me, *"Kan niet lopen"* and she stopped, looked at me, and said something in Dutch that I didn't understand. Then she stopped a man passing by and said something to him. I made out the word *ambulance.* I repeated, *"Kan niet lopen"* and kept on marching. People stopped and stared after me, but I kept on marching—one street after another—weeping. I did not know the reason, yet I did know. My tears were Baby's tears as he lay by my side on the hutch-planks. And they were my own, as I was moved to tears by the streets of Holland, taken along in an Auschwitz labor crew and murmuring to the passersby, "*Kan niet lopen*." They did not know I loved them; they did not know that I wept from an overflow of grief and from a tenderness of soul. They did not know it was Auschwitz weeping and did not know that somewhere, in his place of concealment, God was weeping for Auschwitz and his tears were running down the eyes of a man, his handiwork, marching on from street to street, longing to embrace every passerby, murmuring, "*Kan niet lopen*," weeping in the arms of a stranger, and saying only, "*Kan niet lopen*," not another word, for I did not have another word, nor will another word ever come to me. I am mute, deprived of the word.

GATE THREE

מִבֶּטֶן שְׁאוֹל שִׁוַּעְתִּי
שָׁמַעְתָּ קוֹלִי: יונה ב ג

*Out of the belly of the netherworld cried I,
And Thou heardest my voice.*

Jonah 2:3

GATE THREE

(Prof. Bastiaans recording:)
LSD treatment of Mr. De-Nur,
Session Three,
at my clinic,
Psychiatric Department,
State University, Leiden.

The nurse brought in a drink in a dark bottle for Prof. Bastiaans, and left. Prof. Bastiaans set up the recorder and prepared the syringe. He radiated kindness while I shook with fear. I clenched my teeth to muffle the sound of their chattering. I made an effort to steel myself. This was something else I'd asked other patients about. No, they didn't recall any shaking or tremors before the shot. Sweat—yes, but not much—and after the session, not before. Electric jolt? Yes—right through their bodies when the professor brought them back. But theirs was nothing like mine. Nothing like mine.

I tried everything I could think of to relax. Why was I frightened out of my wits, I asked myself. I'd see the Rabbi of Shilev again, my bit of sunlight in Auschwitz. And if I got used to the LSD, I'd be one step closer to my encounter with my nightmare secret. For God's sake, why panic?

After Auschwitz I saw films and photographs of the hell: piles of corpses, pits overflowing with skeletons, and I was unmoved. At times I wondered at my indifference. Wasn't this Auschwitz displayed before my eyes—the barbed wire fences and over there, look, the watchtowers! These were no studio sets; they were

55

shot on location. It's true the timeframe was post-Liberation, and the cast of agreeable and unmolested inmates peeking out from their three-tiered hutches in the barracks was, needless to say, made up of those who made it through. There were no cameramen in Auschwitz. Still, the actual locations were real, and the pits filled with skeletons were real. Even so none of those things did anything to me. So why—all of a sudden—did I get the shakes? It was crazy! I should have gotten over this craziness first and only then come to Bastiaans. My mind ran riot. I felt the thoughts jetting through. I could still cancel the session...

"Relax, Mr. De-Nur. Your wife showed me your definition of alexytemia[17] and I must admit that in only a few words you hit the target. You must of course know—"

And suddenly_____

the watchtowers stab the dawn sky and the cobalt blue of the heavens bear down on me. Lined up among the other inmates of Block 14 on the parade ground, I wonder how it is that standing here next to my barracks my head touches the sky. Morning roll call will be soon. They chased us out of the barracks in the middle of the night. I can't figure out why my bare feet don't feel the cold. I have a dim memory of learning that at this time of day frozen ground scalds bare feet. This is verified by the sight of everyone around me hopping, foot up, foot down, as if they were standing on hot coals, while my bare feet,

---

[17] alexytemia: the inability to verbalize the trauma, the dominant symptom in Prof. Bastiaans's Concentration Camp Syndrome.

motionless, do not feel the bite of the frost at all.

The sky's light surrounds me thick as mud, and I am inside it, am standing in a pool of it, heavier than the heaviest of waters of the Dead Sea. I can't move. I stare up at the watchtower, never having understood just whom they watch. Who would run away? Where would an Auschwitz Jew run to? Germans inside, Germans outside. What's the point of running away from Germans inside only to run into Germans outside? In fact, they have delivered us from the outside, that outside where not a Jew was left to run to and hide. Besides, outside a non-Jew would promptly hand you over to the Germans and the Germans are everywhere. I ask myself whether there are Germans beyond the crematorium, on the other side, in heaven too.

I stare at the Germans climbing into the cobalt of the Auschwitz skies, climbing up the ladder to the watchtowers, whose turrets pierce the dome of dawn. Shadow-figures ascending the ladders heavenward like angels climbing Jacob's ladder. I wonder how those shadows manage to move in this not-light from the sky, while I am imprisoned in that same light. It's crystal clear to me that this is Their world, Their planet, Their natural law, and this is Their sky. I'm a witness while reciting aloud the verse from the Torah, the way my childhood rabbi had taught me at the age of four: "And he dreamed, and behold a ladder set up on the earth, and the top of it reached to heaven: and behold the angels of God ascending and descending on it." I keep reciting this and want to run to the planks and shout at the Rabbi of Shilev who lies there, "The rabbis made a fool of me!"

My childhood rabbi had taught me this verse at the age of four and then asked me: "My good little boy, where are the angels?"

"In heaven!" I responded.

"Very good, my child. And which floor do you live on, my good little boy?"

"On the second floor," I responded.

"Very good. And if you want to come to the heder from your home, what do you have to do, my good little boy?"

"I have to open the door and go down the stairs in order to come to the heder."

"Very fine. So why is it, my good little boy, you don't ask: if the angels live upstairs in heaven, why does the Good Book tell us that Jacob sees the angels first ascending the ladder and only then, descending the ladder? How come? It should have been the other way around, shouldn't it? He should first have seen the angels descending, shouldn't he?"

"Rabbi of Shilev! Rabbi of Shilev!" I cry out to him, "The Germans are ascending ladders to the heavens! I saw them with my own eyes! They are ascending to take over heaven!"

The Rabbi of Shilev sits on the planks, his stretched legs close together as if he were immersed in the Eighteen Benedictions[18]. Suddenly his face takes on the features of Vevke the cobbler, and I ask: "But Vevke, I saw you lying outside on the heap of corpses behind the barracks."

---

[18] Eighteen Benedictions: the central prayer of the Hebrew service, recited three times daily.

"One moment I am Abel, brother to Cain," Vevke replies, "one moment I am being bound to the altar; one moment I am crucified in Jerusalem, and one moment I am Reb Nachman the Bretzlaver; one moment I am Vevke with the cobbler's bench, and one moment I am the scab-faced Rabbi of Shilev."

"Rabbi!" I cry. "It's not the angels descending from heaven. Come and see for yourself. It's the Germans. They are the ones ascending the ladders up to heaven from the earth of Auschwitz. Rabbi! Rabbi! Are there Germans in heaven too? Even after the crematorium? S.S. men—even there, in heaven too?"

"Tell me, Mr. De-Nur, tell me . . . what—do—you—see . . . see . . . see?"

I hear the voices as from echoing distant skies, thunders rolling down and falling apart; and I'm staring at the Rabbi of Shilev's face whose skin peels away, like brittle bark. An odd affliction, that peeling skin which sparkles in bizarre hues of quartz, yellow-white, and purple.

It's dark on the planks of our hutch and the Rabbi's face radiates through the crusts of many colors. My heart is ripped in pieces, I can see its shreds. Each shred has a face, eyes, mouth, and each addresses me, saying: in the next *selektion* the Rabbi of Shilev goes to the crematorium! I feel that the rabbi could be saved if only he had more sugar in his blood. "One moment I am Vevke the cobbler and one moment I am the Rabbi of Shilev . . ." Vevke was crucified on the brick

59

stove of barracks 14, and then he was sacrificed as a burnt offering. "Rabbi! Rabbi!" I cry out, "Who are you leaving us with? Rabbi, why do you keep silent? Look— Germans are taking over heaven too! I saw them with my own eyes—"

"What do you see, Mr. De-Nur? What—do—you— see?"

I see Nucleus rising out of the crematorium smokestack and soaring to command the heavens. I see great multitudes ascending to heaven up the ladders. Rabbi, who are you leaving us to? Rabbi of Shilev, into whose hands are you abandoning us?"

Just a little sweetness in his blood, they say, could save the Rabbi's life. I'm off to the kitchen barracks, Rabbi! There's a full cup of Kapo Vatzek's marmalade on the window sill of the scullery. I'm off, Rabbi, to steal that cup of marmalade for you. God is at war with the Amalekites![19] They rise up to wage war against the God of Israel, and you keep silent, Rabbi? You sit around on these planks, Rabbi, like a leper and a beggar under Titus's Arch in Rome, awaiting the *selektion* and say nothing? God's at war with Amalek, and you shrink like a withered tree?"

"See for yourself, Rabbi! The barracks is packed with skeletons. Any moment now they'll take us by the truckload to the crematorium. Did Jacob wrestle with the angel for our sake? Let me into the secret, what was the angel after? Think, Rabbi—any moment now our bodies will be fuel to the

---

[19] Exod. 17:16 — "God will have war with Amalek from generation to generation."

furnace for Ashmadai's ascent up the smokestack to heaven. We will be the kindling for his war against the God of Israel. Who will be left, Rabbi, who will remain?"

Deep within the mammoth truck I discover the coalbin, and see you, my rabbi and mentor, turn your face away from me and join the skeletal flow pouring out of the truck into the furnace. And I stand and stare and see my own face up in the sky, wearing the S.S. cap superimposed on a swarm of vipers. I am terrified of that S.S. man—he is me—and I cry:

"Rabbi of Shilev, whom did you leave us with? Who will wrestle with the angel? I beg you, Rabbi, let me into the secret of the angel who wouldn't reveal his name to Jacob! Was Jacob himself the angel? Did Jacob wrestle with himself? And like me, didn't he know his own name? Is the fear that struck Jacob wrestling with himself the same fear that strikes me, seeing myself in that S.S. cap? Let me in on this awesome secret, Rabbi! The battle is being waged in the skies of Auschwitz. I am on my way up to the front! God is at war with Amalek! I'm on my way up...up...up!"

... Until I come back to collapse in my body, coalescing with myself ...

I opened my eyes. The professor's face was all kindness. There was empathy in his eyes as he comforted me quietly: "You must rest now, Mr. De-Nur."

I gasped for breath, like someone stopped in the middle of running crazily for his life. I had lost my breath racing up a stairway that floated in the air. Way up...way up...my last ounce of strength. I hurt; my leg muscles, my entire body—one cramp.

In my heart I was grateful to Prof. Bastiaans for having awakened me and stopped me just then. If he hadn't, my soul would have deserted me while I was running. What had happened to me was just what the books had warned about: Only use LSD with an expert guide to keep you out of harm's reach.

Throughout this re-entry I hadn't noticed Nike sitting behind me in the dark room, trembling with anxiety. She had been invited by Prof. Bastiaans, who needed her there to translate my occasional descriptions of visions in Hebrew.

I stayed in bed for two days, sleeping most of the time, and then decided to take up residence in the clinic community. So far I had been classified as an "outpatient"; this too had made me odd man out. By being a nonresident, placing myself on the sidelines of the clinic process, I missed out on a lot.

I leaned against a tree on the grass in the woods surrounding the clinic: a lovely autumn day. Quite a few patients had come and gone since I'd arrived. I'd witnessed their faces light up as they got the good news that they were on their way home the following day. "The professor okayed it!" was the magic password. It meant, you were fine, cured. More than once I found myself yielding to the temptation to follow such a freed bird and ask, "And how does it make you feel?"

"What do you think? I am the happiest person in the world!"

I sensed the stupidity of my question. No one could miss the happiness shining from my respondent's face. Usually he or she was already bustling about, making ready for departure, but I didn't leave. I clung, out of a need to be close, even if I had to give up my questioning. I suppose I was wearing the same euphoric smile in empathy with the departee's triumph, while my gut was heavy with the desolation I carried wherever I fled. The tormenting nightmare wouldn't leave me. I was familiar with both nightmare and resolution. And I also began to realize deep inside that no one but myself could set me free.

I was sitting in the woods, my thoughts drifting, when I saw Professor Bastiaans leave the street that ran along the woods to his office and come towards me.

"How have you been, Mr. De-Nur?"

I raised my eyes to him. "Just sitting here, ecstatic over the view," I said, intending to rise.

"Please, don't get up on my account, Mr. De-Nur."

I continued, "Just sitting here ecstatic over the lovely view and tempting Providence." I proceeded to share with him the Talmudic sage's maxim concerning the wayfarer who studies Torah as he roams. He'd be tempting Providence if he stopped studying the Torah and spent his time in raptures about the loveliness of this tree, or yonder fold of the field.

Joy welled up in me over this chance encounter with my professor. We strolled along side by side through the trees till we came upon two chairs that seemed to be waiting for us. He sat down, setting his briefcase down by the legs of his chair. "I think I too would like to tempt Providence," he said. "The Torah in my office can wait a bit while I get my share of the view."

I eased into the other chair. I felt a new intimacy with this man and asked, "How is your son? Does he write to you from Tel-Aviv?" I told him the story of how I had come to meet his son, also a psychiatrist, a convert to Judaism, who had settled in Tel Aviv with his Israeli wife. Before leaving for Leiden I had phoned his home for some vital information about the clinic and talked to his wife, who refused to put me in touch with her husband, because she thought I was just one more neurotic or some eccentric—and I could not bring myself to tell her my pen name, a name she would have recognized immediately. It wasn't long, however, before her husband came rushing over to my house and offered an embarrassed apology for his wife's behavior. He had been informed of my identity by a fellow psychiatrist to whom I'd afterwards turned in search of information about the clinic.

Why hadn't I said who I really was? Why didn't I introduce myself to her by my well-known pen name, if only to prevent her from confusing me with the eccentrics who were always calling?

Prof. Bastiaans didn't take his eyes off me. When I finished he said, "I must say I agree with my daughter-in-law, Mr. De-Nur. Why didn't you introduce yourself as the writer? I understand you were making a request or an enquiry, and it's common practice, isn't it, for a person to introduce himself by the name that the other party will recognize. Have you ever considered why indeed you can't bring yourself to say aloud the pen name that has made you so well known? After all, it left its brand on your arm and is nothing to shy away from. Have you ever asked yourself why you sign your books with a number? I'm sure you have seriously pondered the matter."

I looked into the compassionate face of the man sitting across from me, and agreed. His questions gripped me like tentacles. Although I kept trying to ignore them, they held on. And indeed, why was I incapable of saying the name that would have solved immediately any problem I encountered? Moreover, my behavior constantly created a barrier for myself and others. I was the needy one, and yet it absolutely barred me from spending a moment on normal phone procedure. I made a man who owed me nothing, a busy man, drop his work and come rushing to my doorstep to beg forgiveness. What was I doing and why? I didn't intend to do it, but ... I had no answers for these unavoidable questions. Haunted by the shame of it, perplexed, I stared into Prof. Bastiaans's face and said nothing.

"Are you aware, Mr. De-Nur, that you've not been acting like a patient at all? I haven't forgotten your first words in my office about letting you go in while I wait outside. I agree there are times when a doctor must adapt himself to a patient's wants, particularly since we're still in the process of plumbing the workings of the human psyche. We are all groping in the dark, and all we can do is try: try to listen and observe. Try, Mr. De-Nur, this is all of the Torah, in a word."

I looked at the man in his overcoat, sitting across from me, his briefcase on the grass at his feet; the man whose vocation it was to burrow into the center of the dark mountain, to clear a path to souls fallen from that other planet called Auschwitz. For two whole years I had refused to come and take what he had to offer, thinking, "What the hell does _he_ know about Auschwitz?" Now I sat drinking his words:

"After our first LSD session I read one of your books," he continued, engrossed, "and needless to say, on the conscious and unconscious level, nothing is as truthful as what emerges from the heart of a writer bearing witness in a book like yours. When I came to the passage where you tell about squeezing into the coalbin and then emerging from it, so many things I hadn't previously made sense of started coming together. Answers began coming to questions I had put to you with no results. The answers, you see, are still sealed in an embryonic state inside that coalbin, whether you realize this or not."

"To the best of my understanding," he continued, "this coalbin you emerged from into the world of the living is for you not a coalbin at all. Your act of emerging from that coalbin imprinted your every cell with the consciousness that you were then and there being born: in fact, an infant fully gestated and now leaving darkness for the light of day. At that moment, the instant of exit, your soul proceeded to split. On an organic level you knew that you had left the darkness of that coalbin to be reborn. With the coming of liberation you accepted it. Of necessity, as a natural inevitable result, your irrevocable vow not to abandon the man-born-of-coalbin evolved from organic knowledge. In other words, the name De-Nur is proscribed from appearing as author of those books of testimony. In your own eyes, you would be not only a charlatan, but a grave robber, stealing sacred objects from a tomb accursed by the gods. And right here is your opportunity to discover the answers to all my questions. If you enter this coalbin, the womb of your rebirth, as into your soul, you'll find the answers waiting."

I suddenly thought, "Enter the coalbin as into my own soul." Then I am also the coalbin.

Something had been brewing within me since that chance encounter with Prof. Bastiaans. "Right here is your opportunity to discover the answer," the professor had said, and he walked away, leaving me among the trees, looking inward. I had barely taken that first step across the threshold and already there was no turning back, no reneging on myself. "At that moment, the instant of exit, your soul proceeded to split." My heart pounding in my eardrums sounded like Carl Jung's "cry of the unconscious, announcing its existence." Since my exodus from that coalbin just outside the confines of Auschwitz crematorium, my life has been one long confirmation of the ideas of both Jung and Bastiaans. Now I added Fritz Perls to my inner life: "Then I am also the coalbin."

Abrasha's face appears before me, accusing as it never was in life, silent and accusing, and guilt burns in me like fire.

Together we had crossed the river bordering the occupied zone near Graz, Austria. During the war years Abrasha had hidden in a cesspool on a Polish peasant's farm. Only at night, when the peasant was fast asleep, would Abrasha crawl up from the pit like a rat and prowl the fields for something, anything, to eat. After that there was never enough air in the whole world to blow away the stench in his nostrils. From then on every breath he took made his upper lip curl upwards, as if for him the world retained its stench.

The only thing that kept Abrasha clinging precariously to life was his story, the story of his years in the shit pit. It was a memorial to the little Jewish town where he was born and lived and to its inhabitants, all of whom perished, including his own family.

"I'm the last one left of my whole little town," he said, "and it is up to me to create this memorial. Then I can die in peace." Since he knew no Hebrew, I accompanied him to the Hebrew publishing house whose address he carried in his pocket.

When the managing director and founder of the publishing house heard the subject of the manuscript I handed her, she wouldn't so much as give it a passing glance. She only announced, unequivocally, that since the recent publication of *Salamandra,* there was nothing more to say on the subject.

I protested feebly. "No one else except the man in front of you can write what is in this manuscript."

"My dear sir," the woman said. "I don't know whether or not you've read *Salamandra.* I have, and I must reiterate that, on this subject, not one detail could be added. We publishers are no more than middlemen between author and reading public and, don't you see, these days the market is flooded with *Salamandra.*"

A few days later I learned Abrasha had died alone.

As for his unique manuscript, it was posthumously disposed of with the rest of the kitchen garbage. And since then, Abrasha's face comes to me, silent and accusing.

Good God, why didn't I take his manuscript to my own publishing house? Why didn't I simply offer it to the people in charge, introducing myself as the best-selling author of *Salamandra?* That could have opened the door for Abrasha's manuscript. Without a doubt they would have read it and seen its value as a documentary of a unique personal power.

What was wrong with me? Why did I fail in this task? What stopped me from doing what I wholeheartedly set out to do: to be this manuscript's godfather, doing everything I could for this fragile life story that had transcended its own burial in the shit. But such success was not to be for Abrasha. Instead, the same fate was meted out to both life and manuscript. So, in the name of the Lord, who was to blame? Who should shoulder the guilt?

Abrasha's face is silent, accusing.

Over one hundred witnesses gave their testimony to the Jerusalem court at the Eichmann trial, and of them all I was the only one stricken with paralysis. It was because of the judge's main line of questioning:

"Is your name De-Nur, sir?"

"Yes."

"Then why do you hide behind another name in your books?"

A routine question, ostensibly, but the moment it flashed into my brain all hell broke loose. Not only did they want me to melt the two identities into one, but they wanted a public confession, an open declaration that this was so. Escaping to no-man's land was my only solution—becoming a vegetable in a hospital ward. How did Prof. Bastiaans put it?" "At that moment your soul proceeded to split."

The number on top of this page of manuscript has just jumped out at me. I can't believe my eyes: I've filled dozens of folio pages with tiny letters without even realizing the newness of what I'm doing: I am writing in the first person! Until now, all of my books have used the third person, even though I've had to go through contortions doing so. All I've ever written is in essence a personal journal, a testimonial on paper of I, I, I: I who witnessed ... who experienced ... I who lived through...I, I, I, till half through a piece, I suddenly had to transform *I* to *he*. I felt the split, the ordeal, the alienation of it, and worst of all—may God forgive me—I felt like the Writer of Literature. But still I knew unless I hid behind the third person, I wouldn't have been able to write at all. And lo and behold, here I am in the thick of the manuscript and totally unaware of how naturally I am allowing—from the first line onward—the connection with *I*. How did I miss this until now? And why now? Now, after going into the description of my two days of fitful soul-searching in the woods around the psychiatric clinic. "Right here is your opportunity to discover answers." No sooner have I stepped beyond the threshold, arriving at the events of those two days, just passed, and the revelation is there, staring me in the eye. Without the shadow of a doubt I can at last acknowledge my two identities, co-existing in my body.

Two more days of feverish thinking. Then I rushed into the secretary's office blurting, "I'm ready for the session."

GATE FOUR

עוף אחד ושמו חול –
אלף שנה הוא חי ובסוף אלף שנה
אש יוצאת מקינו ושורפתו
ומשתייר בו כביצה וחוזר ומגדל אברים וחי

בראשית רבה, י"ט, ה'

A bird called the Phoenix--
one thousand years it lives,
and at the end of those thousand years,
Its nest is engulfed in flames, and consumes it.
But the germ of its essence survives
and renews itself and lives.

MIDRASH RABBAH, GENESIS 19:5

GATE FOUR

(Prof. Bastiaans recording:)
LSD treatment of Mr. De-Nur,
Session Four,
at my clinic,
Psychiatric Department,
State University, Leiden.

Suddenly_____

The voices issue forth from the loudspeaker like intertwined white-hot chains. Colored purple by the sun, the voices flow from the loudspeaker to my ears, to fill the vacuum inside my head. Whatever was the content of my skull up till now is floating outside of me, before my eyes. And the screaming voices hammer into the void of my skull: "All non-Jews fall out!!!"

I see the faces of Hitler's warriors for the first time. I hear for the first time the harsh screams of the German order:
"Nicht Juden austreten!!!"[20]
My town.

---

[20] *"Nicht Juden austreten!!!"*: "Non-Jews step forward!!!"

The first Polish town bordering on Germany.

My town. No longer recognizable, two days after the outbreak of World War Two.

All of the town's male Jews, gathered into a single group, are a lone sheaf left standing in a stubble field otherwise flat from horizon to horizon. I can see the rope belt girding them together, a belt woven of heartquake, entwined with the ember-glowing words:

"Nicht Juden austreten!!!"

Selektion!

A hand reaches down for me from above, jerks me by my hair out of that sheaf, and as I am plucked aloft and looking down I see the gap my absence has left in the heart of the sheaf.

I was plucked out to dig.

I am digging a grave. Facing me stands the Jew in his prayer shawl and tefillin. The German, his pistol cocked, waits for his comrades to gather and immortalize this scene, a picture souvenir.

I am digging a grave.

The sun-disc shines on the shovel's blade. With every thrust into the earth I bury the sun, and after I fling each shovelful of earth away, the sun glitters once more on the shovel, shinier than ever.

I am digging a grave. The digger who preceded me wasn't fast enough. The German took the shovel from his hands: "Let me help you. Let me show you how to dig. Watch this!" Glittering with sun the shovel's blade smashes right into the mouth of the laggard.

"This is the way to dig!" And the blade lands smartly full force in the laggard's face. And again. And again. And again: "This is the way to dig!"

The likeness of man. Shreds of flesh and no more will appear in the photograph.

I am digging a grave.

Instinctively, I stop the shovel just above a little worm. It writhes around wild with terror at my poised shovel. From the earth the worm cries up at me: "I am life! I am life! Live!" it cries up at me. "Dig and stay alive! As long as your hands keep digging, you live!"

Opposite me stands the Jew in the prayer shawl. The tefillin on his forehead is not a box but a tri-crested crown. The Germans, clapping their hands, cavort around him—the pivot, the silent suspended center—and crown the Jew's head with thorns. They sing his praises: "Hosanna![21] Hosanna! Oh King of The Jews!"

I watch the tefillin on his forehead rise beyond the crown of thorns and open like the doors of the Holy Ark. The tefillin's inner parchment unfurls, its letters one by one cutting themselves adrift to hover about the Jew's head like a glowing marquee: *"Shma Yisra'el, Adonai Eloheinu, Adonai Ehad!"[22]*

The skies ignite, but darkness is on the earth, despite the burning heavens. The flames shoot ever upwards. All at once lightning streaks down from heaven, setting fire to the lone sheaf in the field, turning it into a torch. A hand reaches down and

---

[21] Hosanna: (Heb.) Save us!

[22] *Shma Yisra'el, Adonai Eloheinu, Adonai Ehad:* Hear, O Israel, the Lord our God, the Lord is One.

grasps this firebrand to kindle Abel's offering. The burnt offering exudes a fiery glow into the dark. In heaven a chimney opens to receive the smoke of Abel's offering as it ascends ever upward into the all-consuming void.

Cain's upward gaze is riveted on the opening in the heavenly chimney, on the fiery glow of Abel's offering; on the flaming torch of Jews that is in the empty field of the border town. His hand sweeps up into the salute: *Heil Hitler!*

I see Cain's fist lifted toward the chimney that stands open in the heavens and I sit by the flickering candle, sitting in the Yeshiva of the Sages of Lublin. By my side is Pinni, one of the three chosen by Rabbi Shapira to delve into the Cabala[23] every Thursday night till the break of dawn.

Tonight Rabbi Shapira is with us in person. The Zohar, the Book of Splendor[24], is spread before us. We pore over the weekly Torah portion in Genesis: "And it repented the Lord that He had made man on the earth, and it grieved Him at His heart..."

The bare candle radiates its light only onto the book open before me on the table. Otherwise, the spacious hall is steeped in darkness, and Rabbi Shapira, a white figure in a long linen cloak, paces the hall's length throughout the night. We students are soundless. I see not the shadowy wall but the Rabbi's silhouette, in his white cloak, a white column, drifting back and forth from

---

[23] Cabala: Jewish religious philosophy enthusiastically adopted by Christian humanists during the Renaissance, based on the mystical interpretation of the Scriptures; not revealed to all and sundry.

[24] Zohar, the Book of Splendor: the textbook of the Cabala.

darknes to darkness. All night long, all night long. His white image, filled with the night, lights for me passages from the Zohar, the Book of Splendor.

"And there were giants on the earth in those days—they are the demons Aza and Azael."

"And the Lord said, I will destroy man whom I created."

I see Cain installing a chimney to jut from the abyss to opposite the heavenly chimney that had opened to Abel's offering.

Pinni sits by my side and as my finger guides him through the Zohar, my eyes ask whether he, like me, sees Aza and Azael in Auschwitz transcending the crematorium chimney to announce Nucleus their king, Master of the Universe.

I look at my friend Pinni and see him in the camp at Niederwalden, throwing himself at the barracks chief's feet: "Oh merciful Chief, sweet Chief, grant me the flogging instead of my father!" And his father, sentenced to be flogged to death, screams at his son, "Pinni, away from here! For my sake—honor thy father! Away! Away! Away!"

Pinni the student, called by the head of the Yeshiva, Rabbi Shapira, "the splendor and glory of the Sages of Lublin," Pinni the son, surrendered his soul to the chief's cane. His father, Yellow Itche-Meir, a pious and God-fearing man, refuses to recite the mourner's Kaddish[25] for his child, claiming, "Pinni didn't die! Pinni went straight to heaven in a chariot of fire alive like Elijah. There's no Kaddish for Pinni! No Kaddish for the prophet Elijah!"

---

[25] Kaddish: Jewish prayer for the dead.

My finger is on the Book of Splendor, touching the names Aza and Azael in large bold letters. I cry out to the white figure moving back and forth in the darkness, "Oh Master, my teacher! Don't stand aside! Don't keep silent! Illuminate for your star student Pinni the impenetrable mystery of this passage of the Zohar!"

Pinni's tears drop onto the Zohar open before him. I hold him to my heart, and I hear him whisper, "No redress for me in heaven. I sinned. I broke the Tablets. I violated the explicit prohibition in the Torah about honoring thy father."

Oh Master, my teacher! Your students are going up in smoke in Aza and Azael's chimney. Pinni never even had a taste of sin and you know it! Don't stand aside! Don't keep silent! Decree! You know holy men can issue a decree on their own. You know, if you decree, our Heavenly Father will follow!

Oh Master, my teacher! You must give us the key to understanding. For us the Zohar is a closed book. Why was Pinni made a burnt offering? With my own hands I carried his skeleton to that truck that delivers the dry dead for burning. Oh Rabbi, my teacher!

"What is frightening you, Mr. De-Nur? Whom do you see? Whom are you crying to?"

I cry to the white fire, moving like a pillar in front of me, to my Rabbi, the Master, moving from dark to dark. I cry so that he will take heed of Cain, whose taunting fist is raised at the heavens that opened a chimney to receive Abel's offering.

I cry out to my Rabbi and teacher that he should bear with me, his student poring over the Zohar in the silence, in that dark shit-barracks of Auschwitz, dark except in one corner, where behind a wooden partition a pump gives off the only light, its red sparks shooting upwards as if the engine were going up in flames. Zygmunt Pockface, chief barracks orderly, presents me with two bones, picked clean of meat: "See these? They used to be Benyck, the fat *piepel*[26] 'Holy Father'[27] is in there slicing him up into rations. It's a good deal, this one. No skin off Chief Franzl's nose either. He got himself a fresh piece of warm ass straight from the unloading platform."

I watch the blazing bonfire through the pump cell opening, flames shedding light into the latrine's dark. But Holy Father, seated cross-legged by the fire, has a different face than the one I knew in Auschwitz. His face is Cain's face as he stood facing Abel's offering. And now he sits on the earth with an offering wholly his own, one that Heaven will not reach out to, and feeds the fire with kindling. On his left is a crate filled to the rim with chunk of fresh, raw boymeat. With his long knife he cuts up the flesh, his hand testing each portion for weight, from time to time halving a portion and casting the pieces into the fire.

Lined up along the length of the wall I see human shadows, faces turned toward

---

[26] *piepel:* a preadolescent male inmate used by the barracks chiefs for their sexual perversions.

[27] "Holy Father": nickname for a uniquely cruel hatchetman who was a rank-and-file inmate.

the pump cell opening, delirious in their hunger, in their ravenous fidgety hunger. Faces splashed red by the frolicky fire, their shadows lengthen on the wall until they reach the latrine rafters; their heads flicker on the wall to the dancing rhythm of the flaming tongues.

"Pumf-pumf...pumf-pumf" the heart of the engine is thumping in time with the crackling of the omnivorous fire as it feeds on flesh, blood, human fat, and ordinary kindling.

I stand in the shit-block of Auschwitz in the hush of night, and up there on the wall, beyond the pump cell, I see Holy Father, butcher of Auschwitz, a silhouette seated before the flames that emanate from the nether regions. Around his bonfire, projected on the wall, are the silent, scarlet shadows of humans conducting their shuffling *danse macabre* to the licking, lapping, flapping tongues.

Flames out of the nether regions of Auschwitz. In the fire's entrails is Cain's burnt offering—pieces of boymeat, pieces of an eleven-year-old nicknamed Piepel, the sexual plaything of a block chief in Auschwitz.

The silhouetted arms stretch for a portion, a portion weighed by Holy Father. Overhead:

"Mene, mene, tekel..."[28]

The knife blade glittering in Holy Father's hand sends red sprays of lightning, and the shovel's blade sends sprays of sun. I am digging a grave and hear the worm as it digs

---

[28] Daniel 5:26, 27 - "*Mene, mene tekel...*": "God hath numbered thy kingdom and finished it. Thou art weighed in the balances and art found wanting."

down desperately: "Dig and stay alive!" The Jew in his prayer shawl and tefillin is there across from me, and fear-filled awe overcomes me every time my eyes dare linger on him. I see the Light infinite that the Creator brought into being on the sixth day, the quintessential sabbath eve, and rendered unclarified: the Unknowable creating light unknowable, hidden away for His select few at the end of days. A single beam descends from the cache of light and encircles the crown of thorns that German soldiers have placed on the head of a Jew. I fall prostrate before the power of that light, the ineffable light which no human language can describe. With my face pressed into the earth I offer my prayer: "Would God I had died for thee!"[29]

I get to my feet. And I am he. I am wearing the prayer shawl; to my left arm is strapped the leather tefillin wound seven times. Branded on that arm is my Auschwitz serial number, 135633. This arm disjoins itself and hovers a handsbreadth above the seven revolutions of the tefillin straps. No longer do I feel the earth with the naked soles of my feet: I am dug up by the roots. I cast my eyes down to the patch of earth to which, any moment now, my body will surrender its dying breath, and I hear my soul whisper, "Into your hands I commend my spirit."

A perfect peace wafts down on me from on high as I repay my obligations, one and all. I throw off all the yokes that bear down on my neck. I surrender my body to earth

---

[29] 1 Sam. 18:33.

and my breath to my Creator, while an ineffable light fills me. I haven't known this light since my soul left the mansion of souls, an abode under the throne of Shekhina[30]. I see my soul turn its face toward the source of the light. And all my obligations are repaid, every one.

But I shiver. What of my obligation to Them in Auschwitz? My vow? What of my vow?

And then she enters—the German blonde, the commander of the women's camp where my sister Daniella is interned. She comes staggering to me from the German living quarters. She, out of uniform, drunk and half-naked, prostrates herself at my feet and kisses the hem of my prayer garment, murmuring, "Oh, Holy One! The face of Holy Christ!" I lift my eyes heavenward, wrapping the tefillin strap around my middle finger, as I feel the four Hebrew letters struggling to burst forth from my lips. I check them because the German has finished shooting his film. I see the foreign substance shot from the barrel of his gun as it makes its entrance through the back of my neck into my head, emptying me like a bell bereft of its clapper. I sink to the ground, and the earth reaches out her arms to me, a mother gathering her returned son to her bosom. I see myself shedding my body in preparation for Neshama's flight[31]. I unfurl wings, soaring above the earth's face, up, up. I behold six-winged Neshama making

---

[30] Shekhina: a divine female presence in the Cabala.
[31] Neshama: (Heb.) soul, a derivative of *nesheema*, viz: "And the Lord God formed man of the dust of the earth, and breathed into his nostrils the *soul* of life." Gen. 2:7.

her way to the Source. I accompany her with my gaze and, raising my voice, I call out to her: "And I will betroth thee unto me forever! Yea, I will betroth thee unto me in loving kindness and in mercies!...I will even betroth thee unto me in faithfulness!"[32]

Open your eyes, Mr. De-Nur!

And I'm already back within the boundary of my body.

For the very first time in all the re-entry processes, I wanted to hang on to this shimmering, awe-inspiring vision, which intensified in me in the dazzling noonday light of what I was shown. I was afraid that if I opened my eyes I'd never see Neshama again—she might grow pale, blur, and then disappear altogether.

Martyrdom—death hallowed in the name of God—still possessed me. Days passed and I was still living the vision. The experience wouldn't leave me. Factors and data I had previously been unable to compute were now in the process of coming together, being refined.

I saw Time counter time.

I saw my old-time pal, Pinni, throwing himself at the block chief's feet, pleading to be given his father's flogging. But now, in the vision, I saw myself holding Pinni in my arms, and what I hadn't seen before was becoming my revelation now: my friend's soul. The star of the Sages of Lublin—I saw the face of that soul.

The chief lifted his club and brought it down into Pinni's mussulman-shell; his body, bound as it was to the bench, lay still.

Now, in the vision at Leiden, I saw the face of Death hallowed.

---

[32] Hos. 2:19, 20.

Then, in the German death camp, when I bore Pinni's body to the carrion shed, I looked into his face and at that mouth which had never tasted woman's lips.

Now, at Leiden, I saw his mouth hallowed by the kiss of Shekhina.

Then, in the camp, my tears dropped into Pinni's open eyes, dead eyes fixed on me as he lay, a final rite, in my pall-bearing arms on our way to the carrion shed.

Now, at Leiden, Pinni's unmoving gaze opened my eyes to see the face death hallowed by martyrdom.

I saw them, martyrs all: Rabbi Akiva, his flesh shredded by red-hot Roman iron combs; the masses that the Spanish Inquisitors tossed into their bonfires; the Dutch Jew who would not pour kerosene over a pit full of gypsy children and their mothers. I saw all of them in the pupils of Pinni's eyes.

"Merciful Chief! Sweet Chief! Grant me my father's flogging!"

I saw eye to eye with Nike that it was a good idea for me to stay on in the clinic; I was ripe for the next session.

GATE FIVE

בֶּן־אָדָם !
אֱכוֹל אֶת־הַמְּגִלָּה הַזֹּאת
וָאֶפְתַּח אֶת־פִּי וַיַּאֲכִלֵנִי אֵת הַמְּגִלָּה הַזֹּאת:

יחזקאל ג א ב

Son of Man!
Eat this scroll …
So I opened my mouth,
and he caused me to eat that scroll

EZEKIEL 3:1-2

GATE FIVE

(Prof. Bastiaans recording:)
LSD treatment of Mr. De-Nur,
Session Five,
at my clinic,
Psychiatric Department,
State University, Leiden.

I watched Prof. Bastiaans's solid back as he faced the window, setting up the tape recorder. By now I had internalized our talk in the woods. I had had to undergo thirty years of purgatory before a stranger had opened me to my own feelings—a stranger whom I had obstinately refused to approach for two years, because he couldn't know anything about Auschwitz. Really, what did he know about Auschwitz anyway? But what about when it came down to the *human being* who had been in Auschwitz? He must know how Auschwitz has affected us. No one knows a mind/body system like its owner, except perhaps its explorer, the physician. After a mere two days on my own with the professor's observations, I'd already gotten in touch with some of my feelings. Feelings: long-term residents inside the Auschwitz I had created for myself to fulfill my vow.

"And how are you today, Mr. De-Nur?" Prof. Bastiaans approached me with the needle.

"Excited and scared."

"Normal," he nodded, "perfectly normal."

"I'd like to as a favor, Prof. Bastiaans. I'd like to get together with Prof. Dijkhaus. Would it be too much of an imposition?"

"Oh no, no problem at all! Professor Dijkhaus would be more than happy to oblige."

He was describing in detail his colleague's expertise in theology when—

suddenly_____

the leaves of the tree shimmer in the breeze. They caper in the breeze, radiating a primal green that I have never seen before.

In a medic's white smock—hasn't the Niederwalden camp commander ordained that his medic always wear this white smock?—I perch on top of the sickbay chair so I can see through the square porthole high up the wall. The other inmates are all doing their slave labor detail at the work site. I am the exception, the commander's medic, left behind to administer to a vacant sickbay where no patients are allowed.

Perched atop the chair at the level of the crossbars in the window, I take in the lone sapling left inside the wall. A profound, deeply felt sadness seeps through me for this tender tree kept in solitary confinement. The sapling's loneliness chokes me. Yet, the palpitations of its leaves inside the concentration camp walls is the only vital sign visible. Leaves oscillate in the breeze. These throbs of a living heart send pulses of colors to me, from lushest deep green to yellow, from yellow to blue, from blue to violet. The colors are outside my eyes, while I live their being within me. They pass into me and become one with me. They are a color-streaked torrent rushing into my throat. I gulp the colors raw. Once inside me, each leaf develops its own face, each face staring at me. Here's the face of tailor Zanvil Lubliner, foreman of the ghetto tailor shop. Zanvil, the one who saved me whenever I failed to meet my daily quota: one hundred and fifty buttonholes to be cut and sewn into the uniform shirts of the German *Luftwaffe*; Zanvil, the life-force for us Jews; making us into tailors overnight to keep us out of the onrolling cattle cars earmarked for the Auschwitz fuel factory. His eyes are riveted on me from inside his leaf, making me hear his powerful voice commanding our giant sweatshop from one end to the other: "Jews! Don't stop, sew them their shrouds!" And now the face in the leaf is Tedek's, my sister Daniella's boyfriend in the ghetto. That warm daredevil who one day declared: "Fucking around with the Germans in the ghetto is not my idea of surviving. I'm breaking out of here: through the Carpathian Highlands to Budapest and then to Israel." But Tedek, one foot out of the ghetto, was caught. And from the ghetto—Zanvil, Tedek—now they're all in camp with me. Will they be borne back from the work site tonight on the shoulders of their fellows, in the procession of fallen slaves?

Faces in the leaves, except for a single potato swaying among them—the potato I had earlier saved for Zanvil and Tedek from my daily inmate's ration. The potato swings surrounded by leaves, restless with the mystery of life while its skin flashes at me with stunning brilliance. As I was hiding the potato for them this morning in my hiding place, I saw a protrusion on it like a nipple. Now that nipple tempts me. My hunger is eating me up, squeezing my gut with iron fingers, burning up my brain. The nipple whispers "Come on, just one little bite off me won't hurt them." How can anybody call this just a bite of potato? But it's the same story every day. I focus my outrage on my hunger as I walk over to check on the potato, just a look, no more. Just to make sure it's still protected. My hands move to touch it; I draw it closer to my nostrils for its fragrance. I feel my upper lip slowly explore it and then let my bottom lip have a turn fondling the potato. My teeth weep: "Please, just a nibble." And I allow them their nibble—one bite. And then I go berserk and devour the potato whole.

Not again! Not today too! It can't have happened again. I swore that starting today I'd stay clean. It didn't happen. The whole rainbow of color streams out of the shining nipple directly into my eyes, the nipple is a being unto itself, restless with the tantalizing enigma of life. And I realize that if I so much as take that first step down from this chair to run my fingers over the nipple, I will devour the whole potato. I see Tedek and Zanvil Lubliner, leaf-faces aquiver in the breeze, their eyes on me, while my eyes caress the nipple. Its taste and perfume are like none

I've ever known, like the perfume and taste of Eden's primordial apple, a temptress on the tree of life. "No! No!" I shout at the potato. The belly-dancing nipple taunts me, a naked, snake-like Lilith[33]. My own promise calls me to order, "You are not to touch that potato!" and I scream, "No! No!"

"Who are you screaming at, Mr. De-Nur? Who do you see . . . see . . . see?"

I see the leaf-faces of the people to whom I have this day given my word, my promise. They're my protectors. I tear myself away from the sight of the potato, and see Yaga, the blonde German mistress of the camp commander. She is standing there immobile outside by the wall. Who knows how long she's been out there, eyeing me. I feel the chair sliding out from under me. I grow terrified. I will die for this glimpse I've stolen of the world inside the wall. The rules here are invisible, only the final outcome is obvious. No telling what's permitted and what's prohibited. I let go of the iron bars and am about to leap off the chair when her voice stops me: "Don't hide, Jew! Let me see your face again!"

I've placed myself in mortal danger: she is S.S. commander of the nearby women's camp. Not to follow her order would be a capital offense. I climb back up on the chair and put my head up to an iron-bound square. She's come closer to the window. The color of her S.S. uniform blinds me. She

---

[33] Lilith: the female Ashmadai.

looks up at me and says, "Oh God, it's Christ! It's the sacred face of Christ!"

Standing by my side is Yellow Itche-Meir, refusing to say Kaddish over Pinni, his dead son, while staggering towards me from the cavernous barracks, drunk and half-naked, comes the German blonde. She's been in the S.S. living quarters, where the staff are raping the Jewish girls she's delivered from the women's camp. As a rule, when these orgiastic shouts come bursting out at me from the forbidden S.S. quarters, I spring for cover in the dark between the ground and the hutch planks. Too late. She staggers toward me. She kneels at my feet. She caresses the hem of my immaculate smock, blubbering, "My Savior..."

I'm aghast: When has this march of events happened to me before? In what other life? Clearly I've had this experience before, but when? All I remember is that something horrid is about to happen and the onus is on me to know ahead of time what it is. But then another power takes over, overrides all, and robs me of knowledge of this future that is the past, a future I have already lived. The German blonde kneels before me, coils about my legs and whispers, "Oh my Sacred One!" I turn my eyes to the doorway and see Siegfried, the cruelest of the S.S., Siegfried in hot pursuit of Yaga, panting to carry her back with him. Arms akimbo, capless, shirtless, chest showing through white underwear, he is far more terrifying than in his black S.S. jacket.

"Take him with us," she beseeches him, "I'll do anything you want!"

And, focusing on this very spot in the block, I recall Siegfried's hands killing Zanvil Lubliner here. And I see those hands at the work site killing his minimum quota of one inmate per day.

"Move, medic!" Siegfried commands.

"No! No!" I cry inside. "I won't go! I won't see the specter of my nightmares! No! No!"

"What is it you refuse to see, Mr. De-Nur? What do you see? Tell me, Mr. De-Nur, what do you see . . . see . . . see?"

I see the Voice.

The Voice of God appears to me in the dark of the concentration camp block. The Voice calls out, "What do you see, my Witness?"

I see the Voice.

I see a blaze of glory in the dark of the block. I gravitate towards it while Siegfried leads me there. Being called, I see the Voice, "What do you see, my Witness?"

I see Revelation.

"Tell me, Mr. De-Nur, what do you see . . . see . . . see?"

I see Divine Presence ablaze in the dark of the block, and her radiance blinds my eyes. "How awesome is this block!"

I prostrate myself, Siegfried yanks me up, the blonde S.S. commander entreats, "Be gentle with him, Siegfried, be gentle!"

93

Siegfried helps me up gently and gently leads me by the hand.

"What do you see, my Witness?"

I see the halo of glory in the S.S. quarters. The blaze of glory haloing my naked sister.

I see the blue of my sister's eyes and apocalyptic awe hurls me against the ground.

I see the vision of my sister in a wheel of fire and brightness, and hands of hell wrenching her away from me, away, away and I hear her scream, "Leave me go...he's my brother."

A scream-cloaked cry, red with fire, its flood advancing on me, gushing into me from the four corners of the earth.

And then: darkness.

Darkness enshrouds me as the vocal blur of the camp commander's words crawls through my ears into my brainstem, seeping ever deeper, deeper, digging its way into the center of my skull and taking root there: "Siegfried, stop it! I need my medic! I'm ordering you: Don't you dare shoot him!"

I'm in the snow-covered forest. I come down the tree where I hid during the Death march of the Auschwitz evacuation. My sister's voice wheels like thunder through heavenly spheres, circling, circling: "He's my brother!!!"

I lift my eyes to the voice in heaven and I behold my sister in the flash of sunrise, a nimbus crowning her head. A circle of angels serenade her. Jewish maidens dead by their own hands, eluding delivery to the Gestapo. They sing "Welcome, our sister," and their song has the colors of the rainbow. The colors inundate my palate. I drink them in. The colors pour into my mouth; I swallow them. Angelic songs, with the taste of colors. Rivers of light rush into my eyes. I gaze up at the celestial canopy and hear the celestial choir: "Welcome, our sister!" And the blaze of glory haloes them, wheel within wheel within wheel: "Welcome, our sister!"

But my sister is a sad saint.

I cry up: "Danni! I gave you my word to bring you to the Promised Land!"

But my sister—a sad saint.

I behold *Feld hure*[34] branded between my sister's breasts. And I see myself instantly splitting in two.

I see how I leave my body, separating into two selves: I stand and I stare at my body, in a dead faint on the ground.

"Siegfried, stop!"

I couldn't hear the camp commander's order, then. I was unconscious. Now that I have left my body, I am also able to see the way Siegfried is dragging me by the feet back to the block: I am my own cortege; I am behind my own bumping head. I see Siegfried spitting in my face because he has to drag a Jew instead of shooting him.

I stare at myself, dragged by the feet back to the block and see the key to my nightmares. It's hidden beneath the brand between my sister's breasts. This time I don't fall into a faint, because I've split myself in two. Just as then and now are actually a single unit of time multiplied by two, the *I* of Then and the *I* of Now are a single identity divided by two. I look at my unconscious self,

---

[34] *Feld hure:* (Ger.) Field whore.

and I look at the self staring at my self; I look and see the key to the split.

It stands behind the curtain of the swoon: the secret of the split, deciphered.

I see a heavy drop-curtain of fire and ash being raised, jerkily.

In the depths behind it rises the second curtain, blazing red.

Just behind the second curtain rises curtain number three, bleeding turquoise within flaming blue.

My mother. I see her naked and marching in line, one among Them, her face turned towards the gas chambers. "Mama! Mama! Mama!"

"What-do-you-see, Mr. De-Nur? What do you see?"

A voice comes rolling down to me out of the Auschwitz sky. The echo of each separate word is a hammer crashing on my eardrums.

It's my mother, naked. She's going to be gassed.

I run after her. I cry out, "Mama! Mama!"

I, outside that line, run after her: "Mama! Listen to me! Mama!"

My mother, naked. Going to be gassed.

I behold my mother's skull and in my mother's skull I see me. And I chase after me inside my mother's skull.

And my mother is naked. Going to be gassed.

I'm choking! I'm in the Auschwitz bathhouse. Water came out of the showerheads. Then. Now it's gas. I'm choking harder and harder. The specter of my nightmares is here, staring me in the face. I see it. The secret of my nightmares. I choke inside my mother's skull. I'm in the gas chamber, here inside.

My mother, the most beautiful mother in the world, choking in my vitals, and I am in the Auschwitz gas chamber.

Coiled in my mother's skull, I am tossed into the maw of the crematorium. I burn, burn down to ashes and pass through the crematorial conduit. I reach the core of the mystifying plant of Auschwitz. I see the plant and through its smokestack I rise heavenward.

Still standing by Block 14, looking at the smoke rising from the chimney, I expect to see Mama, Danni, papa in the smoke—since I saw them all in Mama's skull when she was on her way to the gas chamber. And all at once—

It is me I am seeing, risen from the Auschwitz chimney, to my right Shamhazai, to my left Azael, unfurling a majestic canopy over my head. The canopy stabilizes, a mushroom burning against the skies. By blowing horns they declare to the four corners of the earth my new name: Nucleus!

I shake in a maelstrom of awe and panic. Haven't I burned in my mama's skull, and with me my whole family in the Auschwitz furnace? Am I not rising to the seventh sphere? I've already caught up with Mama standing before God's throne of honor. Her shrieks rend the air.

"Take a look at this, God! Take a look!" She pulls seventeen-year-old Daniella out from behind her, ripping open the brand between her daughter's breasts: "Take a look at this, God! Take a look at your *Feld hure!*"

And He looks. God sees.

Now Mama pulls eleven-year-old Moni out from behind her. "Take a look at this, God! Take a look at your Auschwitz *Piepel!*"

And my mama's shrieks rend the air: "Don't you run away from me, God! Look at me, God! They delivered me to you naked, hairless, my children sobbing, 'Mama! Mama!' Did you hear the whimpers of my child, the *Piepel*? Did you hear my child, the field whore, sob? I am the mother of these sobbing children. And you, God, just who are you?"

And He looks. God sees—

me.

He sees how I am seated on my throne under the flaming mushroom while I observe myself standing near Block 14, a skeleton of mussulman in Auschwitz, knowing that I am watching my family in the smoke from the chimney's mouth while my eyes see me: Nucleus! I am Nucleus!

Oh my God!

"What do you see, Mr. De-Nur? Describe to me this frightening sight you see."

It is my own self I see. My own face. Coiled in my mama's skull I was burned and there, joined to the flesh of my family, I was fodder for Auschwitz.

I, the burned one!? I am Nucleus too!?

Oh my God, who is this I standing down there near Block 14, and who is the I beyond there, ruling within a flaming mushroom? When am I up beyond and when am I down below? When are you God the creator, and when are you God the destroyer?

I am below, under the Auschwitz skies. My eyes are lifted to myself between Shamhazai and Azael. I thrust my hands at my self there beyond and hear my self crying bitterly, a wail with no end: "Did these hands, my hands, create you, Nucleus?"

"I'm a human being!" I cry to the S.S. garage superintendent. "No evil spirit! No demon! I am human and I want to live! I am a human being! Human!".

"And how did you get yourself into our garage?" he asks.

"In the truck. The crematorium truck. I hid in the coalbin. Then I got out and I was locked in the garage."

"Stop, Siegfried!" I hear the camp commander ordering him not to shoot me.

"*Ein braver Kerl!*" The S.S. superintendent puts his gun back in its holster.

My bare feet drag along through the snow-covered forest. I know my hours are numbered. I fled to the forest, escaping the Death March, while They were being shot. Now, to return to their midst, I crawl towards their mound of death-riddled bodies. For two years, reckoning by planet Earth days, they passed through me, leaving me behind. Vowing to be their voice, I lived. But now I've given in and join their pile of the dead—a human being, dying.

But gathering the last of my strength I lift my eyes to heaven and gasp:

"E.D.'M.A.! E.D.'M.A!!!"

All the death-riddled skeletons in the pile
burst into a single flame that curls into a
chariot of fire. I, a mussulman, a skeleton
that grows wings; a flaming *salamandra*, a
phoenix raised from my own fire.[35] Like a
missile bound for the upper spheres, I shoot
up from the launching pad of skeletons into
the tempest of my own cry of passion—
And re-enter my body.

---

[35] The *salamandra* was a spirit in Greek mythology who lives in
fire for seven years and then resurrects itself. In Egyptian
mythology, the phoenix was a lone bird which lives in fire for
centuries and then consumes itself only to resurrect itself to start
another such cycle of life.

AFTERWORD AND FOREWORD

And subscribe the deeds, and seal them,
And call witnesses.

Jeremiah 32:44

I was like a tree struck by lightning, standing in flames, and burning.

Nike was anxious about my condition. "We've put in almost an entire year in Leiden," she argued, "and now suddenly, right in the middle of treatment, you decide you're going to run away? Prof. Bastiaans told me again today in no uncertain terms: 'You were there during your husband's last session. You saw for yourself the state he is in. Your husband, Mrs. De-Nur, requires a minimum of two more sessions!' "

I couldn't put it into words. This much I knew: Prof. Bastiaans had accomplished the task I had charged him with. Now that I was rid of the drive that made me force Leiden on myself, I would never make that descent into hell again. From now on survival duty was to be a bearer of testimony in the trial of God vs. Satan—the trial that is being conducted in the heart of man.

101

I'm in Israel. Home.

For the first time in thirty years I go to bed relaxed. Odd sensation, almost unreal; abnormal in its very normalcy.

I'm on the other side of perception's gate and am conscious of my insides churning. Re-evaluation time. Everything inside out. I can accept the throes of my metamorphosis with more grace, now that I'm no longer in the clutch of the specter's claws at night.

But then come the days. Has my night specter gone away only to let day take over?

Before Leiden I was a person split. Inhabited by an inner horror that would burst upon me from under the cover of night. After Leiden, the specter confronting me by the light of day is a universal, even cosmic, nightmare. It was when I called an end to Leiden that I realized the new claims laid on me, claims I acknowledged. Their coordinates were clear, I knew where they were heading. That's why I fled Leiden, back to myself, where all the points converged.

And: I am a tree struck by lightning, standing in flames.

I've gone dry. The insights from my experience in Leiden are so overpowering, constitute a panoramic vision so awesome, that my hand is paralyzed as I reach for the pen. I am trapped in the horror. The word is trapped, burning in my mouth.

So I endure the days and the nights, the months and the years. Like prophet Jonah, son of Amitai, I run away from myself, and to myself I am returned.

Long ago I was a seeker of solitude, distancing myself from human contact and interference, so that I could be alone with Auschwitz. But nowadays Auschwitz has lumbered its way to everyone's doorstep. Wherever there is humankind, there is Auschwitz. It wasn't Satan who created the Nucleus, but you and I. We did!

No longer is the specter a nighttime visitation; it rears up in the light of my days, a vision so horrifying it defies description and disables that hand that reaches for a pen. I am paralyzed. My right hand has lost its cunning.

I work in an orange grove. I find my moments of solace when my grafts take to the trees, like semen fertilizing the womb. There will be life for the old tree in its new offshoots. In addition I keep myself busy with all kinds of writing projects that I never had time for in the past, enjoying the easy glide of my pen on the paper. I also write on a subject they call "the Holocaust." But the moment I focus inward, to that which flows day and night, night and day through my bloodstream, I am trapped in a rolling ball of yarn, a perpetually rolling ball of colored yarn that rolls into my field of vision and looks me in the eye, only to roll away and then come back and then roll away again, rolling endlessly back and forth, forever and evermore. Sometimes the colors of the yarn suddenly separate, and the ball is transformed into a globe, like a globe in a geography class, and it goes a-rolling endlessly into the Unknowable.

From Esalen Nike sends me long provocative letters inviting me to join her in California.[36] Nike believes in power-places. She says she has unearthed several such spots that have been waiting for me, untouched, since the six days of creation.

"Ever heard of Yosemite?" Nike writes. "That virgin forest of mysteries, divinely touched into being. She's waiting to inspire you, waiting to bed you down in a tent all your own, if you would only give her a chance!"

When will Nike ever realize that her man is no writer, certainly not a writer hunting for inspiration. I am more like that dumb animal holed up in her lair, her fetus moving in her womb—a creature bursting to get out of confinement, but finding the passage blocked. With no help in sight this beast crouches in her loneliness, making no sound. Her eyes alone bespeak her pain.

I can't stop thinking that maybe I shouldn't have provoked fate by trying to rewrite my life-script. Maybe I should never have made that trip to En-Dor[37], should never have used LSD to conjure up the secret that a Hand, keeping its own counsel, had cared enough to hide from me.

God
Give me this day the silent word, like
the one
Their eyes gave on Their way to
the crematorium

---

[36] Esalen: A study center for the Eastern and Western arts of spiritual healing in California.
[37] En-Dor: See 1 Sam. 28.

I used to say: Auschwitz is a planet unto itself. There is no rationale to it, no description of it. Auschwitz is holocaust. Holocaust: all cosmic. And Auschwitz has no visitation rights during daylight hours, when everybody's up and conscious. Auschwitz is a night-visitor out of hell; it is the negative blueprint of man created in the image of God.

Like King Saul to En-Dor, I journeyed to Leiden, demanding to be delivered from the Auschwitz of Night. Oh God! Where do I turn now for deliverance from the mushroom-shaped cloud of Auschwitz of Day? From the dreadful vision that stays my hand from transcribing even an iota of it? Its ember sears my lips.

When helplessness gets the better of me, I go over to the drawer, pull out one of the Leiden tapes and turn the recorder on. It no longer surprises me that neither Prof. Bastiaans nor Prof. Dijkhaus could understand these recordings. The words on tape came exploding out of me as encoded pairs whose deciphering required a key:

Auschwitz/Split?

God/Satan?

Other planet/Man?

Questions, questions, questions. And the answer? End!

If only I could put a few lines of the Leiden vision on paper, I could perhaps relax.

I turn off the recorder, put it back in the drawer, and sink numbly into the chair by my desk. I watch the elusive There, that unrevealed There, so incomprehensible, the destination of the endlessly rolling ball of yarn. It's my insides that stare and track the motion of the ball. At moments an object on my desktop will surface from behind There and bring me back to reality, sometimes a pipe, a calendar, a bunch of pens in a holder, or a framed photograph of Nike.

This time, when it's the calendar pulling me back to reality, my eyes freeze on its ciphers: July 2, 1986. I see the date, see time, see the passage of years. And suddenly ... I'm aghast: July 1976! Ten years gone by, ten full years, since Leiden, since Prof. Bastiaans ... my mind goes numb at the mere thought of Prof. Bastiaans. Oh for a few lines of the Leiden vision on paper ....

Usually I counteract this mental numbness by spreading a blanket on the floor and doing a series of yoga exercises. As I straighten the blanket's edges and move into a standing yoga posture, my eye falls on the desk, the pen, and paper. And in this standing position, for the first time, without giving it a passing thought, my hand reaches for the pen, and automatically writes: "LSD treatment of Mr. De-Nur, at my clinic, Psychiatric Department, State University of Leiden."

I didn't notice that I had sat down at the desk, didn't notice that I kept on writing, didn't notice day turning night. I wasn't aware of switching on the desk lamp. On and on and on. Day. Night. One ongoing breath. I must have done all kinds of other things—eat, drink, use the toilet—

I remember nothing of it all.

I wrote *Salamandra* in precisely two and a half weeks. It was my first testimony, written while I was still a skeleton in striped Auschwitz shrouds racing death in a hospital in Italy.

I watch the last line appear on the paper. I turn to stone. I stare at the photograph of Nike on my desk. I am lost to myself. I see nothing real. I rise from the chair.

The yoga blanket is still on the floor, where I had spread it two and a half weeks ago. I make my way to the phone. I dial Nike's university number at Berkeley. I haven't the foggiest idea what time it is there or here. Her voice is on the line and I burst out, "Nike, it's happened ... it's happened, Nike."

But the words choke.

On doubt's tears.

THE DOCTOR'S WORD

In *Shivitti,* the highly gifted Israeli author Ka-Tzetnik 135633 (Yehiel De-Nur) gives us an impressive description, on a conscious as well as an unconscious level, of the mind of a man who narrowly escaped death at Auschwitz. Rarely, if ever, has a victim of Concentration Camp Syndrome—compelled to undergo the intense treatment described herein—been able to recreate this experience for others.

Yehiel De-Nur did not want to undergo this treatment, which he feared greatly. Like many of his fellow sufferers, he felt that any treatment was bound to be ill treatment. It was only at the urging of his life-mate, the Rev. Eliyah De-Nur, that he came to Holland, where I practice as a specialist in the treatment of victims of violence.

I make it clear to my patients that the treatment I offer involves reliving the inferno of their trauma of decades ago, with a difference: this time they will not go

109

it alone in hell. This time, if they consent to the process, they will have a chance to free themselves from the prison of their memory. But the process of surrendering to treatment and yielding control over their own functioning is very difficult, and it is only possible when patients sufficiently trust both the therapy and therapist. With ups and downs, Yehiel De-Nur eventually crossed the threshold to the gates of Auschwitz, and there found freedom.

In words that could not be improved, Ka-Tzetnik 135633 has described his existence in hell—in that near-death proximity to Satan, but also to God. He does not systematically quote all the conversations recorded on the tapes he took away with him, but with great skill conveys their essence in word and image and in a way so expressive and imaginative that the reader must realize just what this human being experienced during the death-years. Never before had he been able to confront his experience on such levels; aided by the treatment, however, he now could. How touching that moment when, ten years later, concluding his self-treatment with the writing of this book, he phoned his wife two oceans away crying, "Nike, it's happened. It's happened, Nike."

After Mr. De-Nur's treatment had been completed, we were out of touch for quite a few years, during which his creative powers gained new strength. In 1987 the Hebrew original of *Shivitti* was finished. At first he was reluctant to publish the manuscript and even thought of burning it. Yet, once published, it soon attracted universal attention.

With great admiration for the De-Nurs, I congratulate them on their success in extracting the very essence of this therapeutic process. In doing so, they make it possible for all readers—for all of us are victims of war—to become conscious of the dimensions and the core of our very existence.

For his commitment, I thank Yehiel De-Nur wholeheartedly.

Prof. Jan C. Bastiaans, M.D.
Oegstgeest, Holland
1989

111

Dear Reader of *Shivitti: A Vision*—

This book has been published by Gateways Books & Tapes as part of a series called Consciousness Classics. These books present ideas and research of lasting value in the field of consciousness. They may be reissues of out of print classics, or classics-to-be, like *Shivitti*, or new works that immediately deserve the status of classics.

Among the Gateways books, *Shivitti* is a unique document of the author's experience of the Holocaust. At the same time, it documents an important contribution to the field of psychotherapy, the contribution of Dr. Jan Bastiaans of The Netherlands. Other Gateways books address related topics such as Transformational Psychology, Metaphysics, Enneagram Studies, Judaica, Fine Art, The Fourth Way, Death & Dying, and Bardo Training.

If you would like a catalog of books, tapes, and other resources—or further information on works available in translation by the author who signed his name Ka-Tzetnik 135633—contact Gateways at one of the following addresses:

Gateways Books & Tapes
P.O. Box 370-SH, Nevada City, CA 95959-0370
phone: (530) 271-2239 or in the U.S.A. (800) 869-0658
email: info@gatewaysbooksandtapes.com
website: www.gatewaysbooksandtapes.com